FEMALE VOICES *in* KEATS'S POETRY

ARGHA BANERJEE

ATLANTIC
ATLANTIC
PUBLISHERS & DISTRIBUTORS

Published by
ATLANTIC PUBLISHERS AND DISTRIBUTORS
B-2, Vishal Enclave, Opp. Rajouri Garden, New Delhi-27
Phones : 5413460, 5429987, 5466842

Sales Office
4215/1, Ansari Road, Darya Ganj, New Delhi-110 002
Phones : 3273880, 3285873, 3280451
Fax : 91-11-3285873
e-mail : info@atlanticbooks.com
web : www.atlanticbooks.com

ISBN 81-269-0174-8

Typeset at
APD Computer Graphics, Delhi

Printed in India at
Nice Printing Press, Delhi

To My Parents

PREFACE

Feminist critics of Romantic verse have often identified John Keats as a sort of a special case, whose poetry, in the light of gender, has been subversive of the traditional conventions of male Romanticism. These feminist critics have repeatedly drawn our attention as to how Keats was branded as 'unmanly' or 'effeminate' by critics of his own time. That Keats is a different case, demanding special critical attention, was set in motion by Susan J. Wolfson's path-breaking essay, *Feminising Keats,* which appeared in 1990. Wolfson and subsequently other feminist critics have pointed out that how Keats's own anxiety, as being perceived as an androgynously passive poet in his own time, tends to merge with the larger issue of the 'more general cultural anxieties about feminisation of men,' in the Romantic period. For eminent feminist critics like Wolfson, Margaret Homans, Anne Mellor and others, Keats becomes a unique poetic personality—full of contradictions and ambiguities, as far as the issue of gender is concerned. An attempt has been made to trace the biographical roots and to probe into some of the ambiguities which tormented the poetic psyche, while inspiring the origin of some of the immortal women figures in Romantic verse.

I am indebted to Prof Malabika Sarkar, Department of English, Jadavpur University for her invaluable suggestions, which helped me considerably in timebound completion of this book. The book has come out with flying colour owing to the advice, interest and encouragement of a number of other people. I would specially like to thank my senior colleagues of the English Department, St. Xaviers College, for their encouragement and timely support. The facilities provided by the National Library, libraries of British Council, Jadavpur University,

St. Xaviers College and Centre for Studies in Romantic Literature are gratefully acknowledged. The word processing facilities provided by M/s OPUS have been of immense help. Finally, I wish to thank my students and those close friends who have always been a source of support and encouragement.

ARGA BANERJEE

INTRODUCTION

This book intends to examine in detail some major women figures in Keats's poetry, especially in the light of recent discussions of sexual ambiguity in Keats. Sexual ambiguity, as scholars[1] have pointed out, refers to the dual sexual identity or the fragmented poetic self as reflected in Keats's verse. The book examines some major women figures of Keatsian verse in the light of this dual strand: first, as to how far these women figures are projections of Keats's own poetic self and secondly, what do they reveal, as regards attitudes of a male poet towards women. Besides focusing on these Keatsian women figures, in the context of sexual ambiguity, this study also examines some other female figures who fall outside the sphere of sexual ambiguity. These figures are examined as they also provide interesting observations on feminine projections from the contemporary male viewpoint. Efforts are also made to correlate the shaping of these attitudes with the psychological and biographical strands of Keats's life. While the analysis focuses on women figures like Psyche on the one hand, it studies fatal figures like Lamia, La Belle on the other. While the former category explores the aspect of sexual ambiguity, the latter group reveals a lot about Keats's complex attitudes as a male poet towards the opposite sex. So indirectly, an attempt has been made to find out to what extent these attitudes of a male poet are unconventional or unique to his age. The aspect of fragmented poetic self or tendency to identify one's self with both sexes in all probability gives rise to a lot of insecurity, complexity and anxiety of the poetic self—especially as regards interaction with the opposite sex is concerned. As to what extent this anxiety is reflected in the portrayal of Keatsian women figures is also another important issue of discussion undertaken by this study.

Keats's early life had a lot to contribute to his sexual ambiguity. Critics and biographers[2] point out that, being extremely close to his mother, he was specially grieved to lose both his parents within a short span of time. Shortly after his father's expiry in an accident, his mother abandoned her children for a second marriage. Losing his mother, whom he had loved so dearly, to another man left him insecure. This basic insecurity accompanied him through out his later relationships with other women as well, resulting in a lot of complexity and anxiety. What definitely exacerbated this insecurity leading to the splitting of the poetic self was his need to play the feminine role of mother in his early life for his younger brothers and sisters. This single factor, pointed out by many scholars, definitely complicated his attitude towards women later in life. In his relationships with women, he was diffident and unsure resulting in complexities—often fluctuating between extremes of neurotic possessiveness to suspicions of great proportions. Scholars also point out, that due to his humble social origin, that he was often subjected to social alienation—as poetry was regarded as the bastion of the elite and aristocracy. Such alienation aligned him indirectly with women in contemporary society, as women then were quite often marginalized. Such a complex network of social and personal circumstances contributed to Keats's low self-esteem and isolation. These factors also made Keats's poetic existence a rather passive one, which according to scholars again, involuntarily contributed to his identification with the opposite sex.

Contemporary scholars of Keats have focused on the feminine aspects of both his life and works and synthesised their observations with feminist insight. The complexity of Keats's sexual ambiguity has evoked varied reactions from critics. They have tended to categorize him both as an early feminist and an opponent of feminism. A scholar like Susan. J. Wolfson, through her study of Keats, investigates various conflicting interests that lie buried in male writing, within nineteenth century patriarchal society. According to her, the sexual ambiguity of Keats, or the fragmentation of self is not merely an isolated case for probe; but in the long-run, it points at the wide 'cultural anxiety' as regards 'feminisation of the male in the Romantic period.' The time when Keats wrote, as gender studies in Romanticism reveal, was a time when 'a determined critical attempt was being made to enforce standards of manly conduct'[3] and behaviour on male poets. So critics like Anne Mellor and Susan Wolfson point out that Keats is often branded as effeminate or his special case inspires for attempts to make more flexible the prevalent notions about masculinity in the Romantic period. Critics like William Hazlitt and Leigh Hunt too have earlier emphasized the feminine traits in Keats. In an attempt to study the Keatsian women figures closely, in the light of sexual ambiguity or otherwise, the book has been divided into the following chapters.

The first chapter examines Keats's personal life in detail, closely assaying the women figures in his personal life in order to trace and assess the psychological roots that have contributed to his sexual ambiguity, insecurity, anxiety and tension in his attitude towards the opposite sex.

The second chapter looks carefully in detail at the concept of sexual ambiguity, as discussed and examined by recent scholars of Keats. Besides exploring the split of the poetic self, this chapter also explores related issues that are triggered off by this ambiguity such as anxiety, helplessness, possessiveness, suspicion, extreme self indulgence or narcissism, poetic transvestism etc.

The third chapter explores women figures which stand as representatives of meek womanhood. The three major women figures discussed in this chapter are Psyche, Madeline and Isabella. Besides the aspect of sexual ambiguity, as and where it is evident, this chapter along with some of the subsequent ones, tries to find out if Keats tended to see or project his women figures in the mould of conventional gender stereotypes or not.

Women in Keats's verse can be destructive and predatory as well. Chapter IV examines three central women figures who are conventionally branded as seductive—La Belle, Lamia and Melancholy. These fatal women figures reflect the anxiety and insecurity that Keats encountered in his own interaction with women. Occasionally these attitudes appear confusing, contradictory and conflicting. While in *La Belle Dame Sans Merci*, we only get a male viewpoint, with the lady's perspective being ignored totally, in *Lamia* we find Keats implicitly condemning the traditional forces of patriarchy that bring about her destruction. Through his fatal women figures, Keats projects conventional gender stereotypes of seductresses—of sexually conscious women, who are a threat to the social code as endorsed by the patriarchal society and they have to be crushed by patriarchal forces through all means. The same element of fatality and anxiety hovers over Melancholy in Keats's *Ode on Melancholy*. But in this ode, the voices of patriarchal authority and condemnation are absent, unlike *La Belle Dame Sans Merci* or *Lamia*.

The fifth chapter examines femininity in *Endymion*. Though chronologically an earlier work, yet *Endymion* provides a complex blending of Keatsian attitude towards women. Endymion represents Keats's own quest for immortality in life. Endymion's attraction to both Cynthia and the Indian maiden represents the personal dilemma of the Romantic Keats, a poet torn apart between worlds of idealism and realism. Cynthia, in a way, represents the culmination of Keatsian narcissism—a pining for a regressive fusing love and towards idealized fantasies of the mother and self.[4] However, the love for the idealized mother image and self ultimately gives way to a realistic acceptance and fulfilment of love through union with the Indian maiden. So *Endymion* provides a complex study of femininity in various ways. In this chapter we witness two kinds of femininity emerging in *Endymion,* one being a projection of narcissism, mother fixation and Romantic idealism, while the other is a more realistic version based on acceptance of femininity as the 'valued other.' Keats ultimately supports the latter and shows that ultimate fulfilment of love lies in embracing of femininity as the 'valued other'—an autonomous, free, independent and different entity and not a narcissistic self projection.

The sixth chapter examines the centrally important figures, Mnemosyne and Moneta in Keats's *Hyperion* and *Fall of Hyperion* respectively.

The concluding chapter draws inferences from observations in the earlier chapters. It sums up what Keatsian attitudes reveal, as far as the opposite sex is concerned, through the study of various women figures in his verse. In this context, it is imperative to underline the fact that due to a complex network of biographical and social circumstances Keats presents a rather complex case especially as regards gender studies. Keats's special case defies any definite categorization or classification unlike his other contemporary male Romantic poets. Keats not only complicates the issue of gender, but also defies the traditional norms of masculinity and femininity—which, quite naturally, subjected him to a lot of hostile criticism during his time. These conflicts, complexities, confusions within his own self find reflection in his female figures of verse as well. They encompass a wide range of complex, conflicting and contradictory issues like narcissism, mother fixation, approving of patriarchal norms, on the one hand, to granting of autonomy and independence to female figures, on the other. Such a wide spectrum of divergent and complex attitudes makes it impossible to draw any definite single inference. However, it provides a unique and interesting probe into the intricacies and complexities of the poetic mind, especially when it comes to relationship with the opposite sex.

NOTES

1. Susan J. Wolfson, Anne K. Mellor, Nicholas Roe, Marjorie Levinson, Margaret Homans, Karen Swann and others.
2. *Critics*: Anne K. Mellor, Susan J. Wolfson, Nicholas Roe and others. *Biographers:* Aileen Ward, W.J. Bate, Stephen Coote, Robert Gittings.
3. Editorial Note to Susan J. Wolfson's essay, *Feminising Keats* in Peter J. Kitson ed. *New Casebooks: Coleridge, Keats and Shelley* (London: MacMillan Press Limited, 1996), pp. 109-10.
4. Barbara A. Schapiro, *The Romantic Mother: Narcissistic Patterns in Romantic Poetry* (Baltimore: John Hopkins UP, 1983), pp. 37-41.

CONTENTS

1

Seeds of Confusion

THE brief eventful life of John Keats (1795-1821) was deeply influenced by women figures around him—be it in the form of mother, sister, beloved or even casual acquaintances. As to how far they are relevant to the myriad forms of femininity we encounter in his verse, is a question that will be taken up later. But a close examination of women figures in Keats's personal life would enable us to trace the psychological roots that have contributed to his sexual ambiguity, insecurity, anxiety and tension in his attitude towards the opposite sex.

There is not much authentic personal record of John Keats's childhood. Being 'born on the last day of October 1795 and christened seven weeks later at the London church at St. Botolph Without, Bishopsgate,'[1] John Keats was the eldest of the five children of the family. While we have greater access to the biographical details from his adolescence onwards, unfortunately our knowledge within authentic means, about his childhood and early years is rather scanty. It was little after a year of Frances Jennings marriage with Thomas Keats that the poet was born.

Of the women figures we meet in Keats's personal life—a figure of profound influence was his mother. Unfortunately when Keats's early biographers were searching for details about her, she became easily vulnerable to gossip and slander. Like John Keats, his mother too, was the eldest of three children of the family. Frances Jennings was only nineteen years old when she got married to Thomas Keats. Gossip prevails about her flamboyant impulsive nature. Most of the distorted biographical details about Frances Jennings were forwarded by Richard Abbey to John Taylor, who thought of writing a biographical memoir after John Keats's death. As John Taylor writes, at a very early age she was keen on marriage.

> ...At an early Age she told my Informant, Mr. Abby, that she must & would have a Husband: and her passions were so ardent, he said, that it was dangerous to be alone with her. She was a handsome, little woman—Her features were good & regular, with the exception of her Mouth which was unusually wide. A little Circumstance was mentioned to me as indicative of her Character—She used to go to a Grocers in Bishopsgate Street, opposite the Church, probably out of some liking for the owner of the Shop—but the Man remarked to Mr. Abby that Miss Jennings always came in dirty Weather, & when she went away, she held up her Clothes very high in crossing the Street & to be sure, says the Grocer, she has uncommonly handsome Legs. He was not however fatally wounded by Cupid the Parthian—
>
> But it was not long before she found a Husband, nor did she go far for him—a Helper in her Father's Stables appeared sufficiently desirable in her Eyes to make her forget the Disparity of their Circumstances, & it was not long before John (Sic) Keats had the Honor to be united to his Master's Daughter. He did not possess or display any great Accomplishments. Elevated perhaps in Notions by the sudden Rise of his Fortunes he thought it became him to act somewhat more the Man of Consequence than he had been accustomed to do....[2]

That there was parental disapproval in Frances Jennings marriage with Thomas Keats is clearly borne out by the fact that there were no relatives on either side to witness the marriage ceremony at the prestigious church of St. George in distant Hanover Square.

John Keats spent his early childhood with his parents at a house in Craven street, north of the City Road. A little over a year after his birth, his brother George was born on 28 February 1797 and Tom on 18 November 1799. By the end of April, on 28 April 1801 to be exact, the fourth child Edward was born. Edward survived barely seven months. It was two years later on 3 June 1803 that the only daughter Frances Mary Keats was born. It was after the death of Edward Keats that the Keats family moved to the Swan and Hoop which was managed by Thomas Keats on a rent of £ 44 a year.

Keats's mother always entertained ambitions of sending her children to Harrow, a prestigious haven for children mostly belonging to the elite sections of the society. As a mother she was affectionate and warm, and her eldest son—John Keats, as his brother George affirmed later on, was her favourite. Writing in 1828 about his mother, George Keats emphasizes her 'doting fondness'[3] for her children, especially John, whose face resembled hers. From his father John inherited his unusually short and fairly stocky structure.

Very few anecdotes of Keats's infancy survive. However, of the surviving anecdotes two can hardly be ignored, especially in the context of a discussion of women figures. A certain Mrs. Grafty, an old lady, on being informed that the baby she knew in infancy was a budding poet, confirmed that from a very tender age, instead of giving direct replies to questions asked, he displayed an innate alacrity to make a rhyme of the last word mentioned to him. The second striking anecdote relates to the intense bonding between the mother and son since infancy. At the age of five, when Keats's mother fell ill and was advised total bed rest, little John was found guarding his mother's bedroom with an old sword. She had a special liking for John and from his early childhood it was reciprocated with ostentatious chivalry by the devoted son. As Stephen Coote puts it,

> …This defiant little gesture may have been characteristic of an infant whose temper was sometimes said to be violent and ungovernable, but it also indicates the passionate

> and even possessive relationship that had developed between the boy and his indulgent mother[4].....

Ever since his childhood, death was a constant companion of Keats. When he was just six years old he lost his younger brother Edward in 1801. However, it was the death of his father that triggered off a chain of calamities for the Keats family. At that time, John had joined his school at Enfield for less than six months or so. On 14 April 1804, his father Thomas Keats met with a fatal accident. It was a Sunday, and he had been on a visit to his children at Enfield. After the appointment he had gone to dine at Southgate. While riding back, rather late at night, his horse slipped on the cobble stones and in a fatal accident cracked his skull. He was taken to a surgeon but he expired the following morning.

The death of Thomas Keats is significant, for it gave a dramatic twist to the domestic life which had a direct bearing upon the children. It threw the entire family into a state of chaos. Due to his untimely death the children lost their inheritance. The death affected Frances Keats as well. It resulted in remarriage of the young widow, following her brief disappearance from the house. All these developments had a silent, yet, great effect on the mind of the children. As Stephen Coote states in his biography on Keats,

> ...The effect on a little boy of eight and a half, the still and chilly fact of the corpse, the pallid undertakers and nodding plumes, the red eyed griefs and sudden solicitudes of his family, must have been one of utter confusion, of fear even beside the cold vault in the church in Coleman Street. Then, in her grief and anxiety, his mother briefly vanished. Her disappearance is witnessed by the fact that when the collector of the Poor Rate called at the Swan and Hoop he found the vague, shadowy figure of Elizabeth Keats (a sister of Thomas's perhaps) apparently in charge.[5]

The situation that Keats's mother faced was a grave one. She had to withstand a wide range of calamities. Thomas had left behind an estate of approximately £ 2000. It was to take some time for legal formalities to be completed so that Frances could obtain charge of the amount, but even when it was available, the interest on the sum was not enough to provide rent, school fees and other expenses of the family. When she returned after her disappearance, 'she took out in her own name a short lease on the livery stables of the Swan and Hoop (but not on the inn itself).'[6] She remarried a couple of months after her husband's funeral on 27 June 1804. The man she married this time was William Rawlings who was then a minor clerk in the company of Smith, Payne and Smiths of George Street, a banking firm. When the children returned from school at midsummer 1804, they found Mr. Rawlings installed as their new father.

What was the impact of his mother's remarriage on Keats? Again we have very little evidence as regards that. But it is certain that the Keats children did not live long with them. They stayed with their grandmother who did not approve of her daughter's second marriage. Whatever may be the time span it is undeniable that,

> …the idealized woman of his crucial early experience, beautiful and recklessly affectionate, had betrayed and abandoned him in a manner beyond his understanding, and forever afterward he was haunted by the fear that any woman he loved would play him false and then leave him. The boy began to develop a wariness in his dealings with others, beneath his instinctive openness and spontaneity, "All my life I have suspected every body." Keats later wrote[7]

However, the second marriage did not last long and Frances walked out of the marriage. Though the exact time is uncertain, within a year's time after his father's death, Keats lost his maternal grandfather John Jennings as well, on 8 March 1805. The will of Jennings created a great deal of ill feeling between Keats's mother, her newly wed husband on the one side and Keats's grand mother and maternal uncle on the other side. The Court Judgement 22 May 1806 declared Mrs. Jennings to be in charge of the stock while the remaining property was to be divided between the mother and the son. The verdict left Keats's mother in a precarious state. Her situation, was further worsened by the failure of her marriage with Mr. Rawlings. While her husband continued to stay at the Swan and Hoop, she neither had money nor anyone reliable to fall back upon. But this precarious state of his mother had a terrible effect on John Keats,

> ...Her plight was indeed pitiful, but the effect on her oldest son was traumatic. The passionate, possessive little boy had lost his father and then seen his adored mother taken, first by another man and then lost altogether. He had been removed from his home and watched powerlessly the destruction wrought by mistrust. Loss and insecurity seemed to characterize every relationship. What was given was snatched away, while, below appearances, flowed the constant, wordless undertow of threat, the seeming certainty of pain.[8]

In these moments of crisis, it was Keats's grandmother Mrs. Jennings who tried to provide a home for the Keats children at her new residence at Edmonton. It was sometime in 1809 that Keats's mother returned to her family. She was a sick woman then and her condition was rapidly deteriorating. John Keats tried to do everything within his limitations of adolescence to ensure that his mother did not leave again. He tried his best to make her feel proud. Returning to his school in January 1809, he carried away all the first prizes in literature. Reading became an obsession for him. He strenuously exercised his mind and exhausted his school library at a swift pace. However, quite unfortunately the mother to whom Keats brought back his coveted prizes with pride was rapidly declining in health. By the end of 1809, it was clear that she had tuberculosis. When the Keats children came back home during Christmas holidays in 1809, they found their mother gravely sick. Keats immediately devoted himself to nursing his mother. He prepared meals for her and gave her prescribed medicines at appropriate times.

> ...Night after night he sat with her as her hacking cough wore her down and her sputum reddened with blood. In

> the quiet intervals, as she slipped away from him again, he read novels to her or merely watched by her bed as she slept.[9]

All these details clearly show that John Keats shared an intense bond with his mother during childhood. We also empathize with the grief he suffered at Enfield when he learnt of his mother's death, in barely less than three months time on 10 March 1810. He gave way to prolonged mourning. His mother's death had a deep impact on him. His robust aggressive temperament gradually changed into a silent adolescence absorbed in his reading. Keats's absorption in study is noteworthy. It clearly shows his recoil from a world which was characterized by death, decay and pain. Happiness and beauty were transient—under the constant threat of death hovering around. It is this ethereal quality of beauty that we find as a recurrent theme in his verse later on. Beauty that is not permanent but 'Beauty that must die' (*Ode on Melancholy*, Stanza III. 21). His devotion to and the subsequent loss of his mother also reflect the bitter melancholia that was to accompany him for the rest of his life.

The death also triggered off the anxiety that constantly accompanied him in his interaction with the opposite sex. The constant fear of loss, betrayal or abandonment found extension in characterizations of his male protagonists in verse—like Endymion, Glaucus, Knight-at-arms and Lycius. Their anxieties seem to be an adult extension of Keats's own childhood insecurity and early loss of parental love. Aileen Ward, Keats's biographer, even suggests that Keats's choice of profession as a surgeon was probably influenced by his mother's death. She feels in exercising his choice, Keats 'was trying to relieve an unconscious sense of guilt for having failed to save her.'[10] Even his decision to become a poet seems to have been an offshoot of his inherent desire to flee from the horrid memory of her sufferings—sufferings which he himself witnessed while nursing his mother on her death bed. The reality was too painful and he wished to flee from it. We are reminded of the lines in *Ode to a Nightingale* that depict the painful reality, the world from which the poet wants to escape:

> Fade far away, dissolve, and quite forget
> What thou among the leaves hast never known,
> The weariness, the fever, and the fret
> ....
> Where youth grows pale, and spectre—thin, and dies;
> Where but to think is to be full of sorrow
> And leaden-eyed despairs;
> Where Beauty cannot keep her lustrous eyes,
> Or new Love pine at them beyond tomorrow.
>
> [*Ode to a Nightingale*. Stanza—III, 21-30]

It is on the 'wings of Poesy,' as we find in the following stanza, that Keats wants to escape,

> Away! Away! For I will fly to thee,
> Not charioted by Bacchus and his pards,
> But on the viewless wings of Poesy,[11]
>
> [*Ode to a Nightingale*. Stanza—IV, 31-33]

The role of mother is crucially important in Keats's life as it is with any other poet. As Barbara A Schapiro, a psychoanalytic critic of Romantic poetry states:

> The image of the woman, whether she figures as an ideal goddess or a serpentine vampire, a deserted woman or, more frequently, as the ever—maternal Nature, is central to the poetry of the Romantics. The relationship with the woman which the poetry either expresses or implies is rooted psychologically in the relationship with the first woman of all our lives, the mother.[12]

The relationship with the mother serves as the core experience in the blossoming of personality and attainment of psychic and emotional maturity. The image of the mother according to psychologists, as represented unconsciously, is greatly internalized in infancy and retained throughtout the rest of life. The unconscious representation owes its origin to the first relationship fantasized by the son with his mother. In the case of certain unavoidable shortcomings of maternal care, psychologists point out, ambivalence characterizes the first love relationship between the son and the mother. In Keats's life, we find such shortcomings of maternal care which definitely contributed to ambivalence in his relationship with his mother as first object of love. When this ambivalence is internalized as was the case with Keats, it results in a split of the self or ego, 'The child internalizes both the "good" loving mother and the "bad," frustrating one![13]' Psychologists point out that if the relationship with the mother is damaged by other allied disturbances like separation, death, or emotional rejection, the internal splitting becomes even more intense. In Keats's case we clearly see that two major factors were present in the form of separation and death. He was not only separated and rejected by his mother during her second marriage, her return too did not last long as she expired from tuberculosis shortly. Such a splitting of self weakens the ego.

> ...Failure to resolve this primitive ambivalence, to integrate the internalized "good" and "bad" objects, prevents both the formation of a mature, cohesive self and the sense of a cohesive, concrete reality outside the self. Such a split internal condition may also result in a regressive desire for refusion with the mother and in a primitive idealization of self and object images. The idealization of the self image compensates for the child's real feelings of deprivation and rage, and the idealization of the parent image compensates for the depriving real parent. These idealizations may combine to form the "grandiose self." And the condition as a whole characterizes pathological narcissism.[14]

A work of art, is an extension of the inner world of an artist. Most of the recent discussions on Keats's sexual ambiguity, which I will deal at length in my second chapter, can be resolved and understood if we try to trace and understand the psychological roots of Keats's relationship with his mother in his infancy and childhood days. Separation and early death of his mother contributed to a split within him. It lead to a series of idealizations and narcissism as well. We find all these traits more clearly in his early works like *Endymion*. I shall discuss these strands in my subsequent chapter on *Endymion*.

The second most striking woman figure in the domestic circuit, especially during Keats's childhood and adolescence was Mrs. Alice Jennings—his maternal grandmother. Whatever loss of maternal affection Keats encountered was largely compensated by his grand mother. After the death of his father, when Frances Keats married for the second time, it was Mrs. Jennings who took charge of the children. She faced the crisis with a great deal of courage and caution. Within her limited means, she tried her best to provide a proper home for her grand children. She moved to a house in Church street, Edmonton, which incidentally was the last real home for the children of the family. Mrs. Jennings poured all warmth and affection within her means over the Keats children. Even decades later, Keats's sister Fanny fondly recollected memories of her grandmother baking a Lancashire cake for them, heavily laden with cherries and raisins.

In the absence of her husband, daughter, sons and son-in-law, Mrs. Jennings was naturally worried about the fate of the four Keats children. She was extremely practical and she tried her best to ensure for her grandchildren whatever she could, within her limitations. Whatever little monetary provisions she had, she ensured it for her grand children. Four months after the death of her daughter Mrs. Jennings passed over to the trustees a large portion of her inheritance from her husband. In her will, she confirmed the appointment of Richard Abbey and John Nowland Sandell as guardians. Richard Abbey took actual charge of the trusteeship after the death of Alice Jennings on 19 December 1814.

Keats's grand mother was a sharp contrast to his own mother. She was bold and efficient, one who retained her strength and presence of mind against heavy odds of life, and tried her best to protect her grandchildren. In a jingle describing his boyhood, which he later wrote to amuse his sister, Keats referred to his grandmother as 'granny good.' Against odd circumstances, she tried her best to provide a little bit of security for the insecure Keats children.

So as far as maternal affection goes, we find that indirectly Keats had two mothers in his childhood—one in his own mother Frances Keats, being young, pretty and unreliable, the other in the form of Alice Jennings—his grandmother being aged, reliable, responsible and affectionate. So as Aileen Ward points out,

> ...it helps to explain a division in his nature which appeared later in many forms, one being a tendency to be drawn towards two different types of women-flirtatious young beauties and serious young ladies, sexually much less challenging, often several years older than himself....[15]

The Keats brothers were fiercely possessive of their sister Fanny Keats and John was no exception. The boys felt a spontaneous pull of affection for their sister, 'Abandoned themselves she was someone they could treasure, indulge and vie for.'[16] The brothers were not only possessive of their lone sister, they competed with one another for drawing more attention from her. Born in the Craven street house on 3 June 1803, she was christened at St. Botolph's Without, Bishopsgate on 17 June as Frances Mary Keats. After the death of her grandmother in 1814, she was under the guardianship of Richard Abbey. She was sent to school for three years after which she was taken in the household of Richard Abbey. Fanny was unhappy at being taken away from school. However, even Keats's own intervention into the matter with Mr. Abbey failed to yield any productive results. Richard Abbey disapproved of her staying in touch with her brothers. In the words of Keats's biographer,

> ...Neither Tom nor Keats had settled to what Abbey would have regarded as decent employment and it seemed to him that Keats in particular was surrounded by bohemian acquaintances while merely squandering his inheritance. A young girl needed to be protected from such wastrels. Besides, on the one occasion when he relented, it seems that Fanny met the Dilkes and late, in all innocence, gave what was perhaps a garbled impression of what happened.

> At all events, the visits stopped. For weeks Keats tried to change this cruel ruling. He went to see Abbey on no less than three occasions, but all he was able to obtain was a promise for one more visit between the beginning of November and the start of Fanny's Christmas holidays.[17]

The deep distrust of Abbey towards Keats prevented the latter from meeting his sister. Keats often had feelings of guilt about his sister and on occasions he even reproved mildly of Fanny's behaviour, asking her to persuade and convince Abbey, that given the opportunity to socialize she had no other option other than being around ailing Tom's bedside.

> …I do not mean to say you did wrongly in speaking of it, for there should rightly be no objection to such things: but you know with what people we are obliged in the course of childhood to associate: whose conduct forces us into duplicity and falsehood to them. To the worst of people we should be open hearted.[18]

Yet retaining his composure against such odds, he counselled Fanny to show prudence and not indulge in duplicity with Abbey. Duty towards Tom too prevented Keats from doing his duty towards Fanny. Yet he tried to write to her as frequently as he could. When Fanny came of age in 1824, she called upon Dilke to act as her trustee. Thereby she forced Abbey to turn over her share of her grandmother's and her dead brother's money. By the end of 1825, Fanny had a fortune of £ 4,500. The following year 30 March 1826, she got married at Luke's Church, Chelsea.

Fanny to Keats was a little frail being to treasure and protect. All Keats letters to her have that predominant undertone of filial affection and bondage. His unalloyed love is clearly revealed in his light hearted doggerel verse '*A Song About Myself*' he wrote to amuse his sister Fanny when she was fourteen years old.

> There was a naughty boy,
>   And a naughty boy was he,
> He kept little fishes
>   In washing tubs three.

In spite
Of the might.
Of the maid,
Nor afraid
Of his granny—good,
He after would
Hurly burly
Get up early
And go,
By hook or crook,
To the brook[19]
……..

Keats was constantly aware of his duty towards his sister and tried his best to fulfil it within his limitations. He seems painfully helpless when he refers to his sister walking about in his imagination on his death bed. Observing Fanny's early life we feel she might have indirectly influenced some of the meek, helpless, vulnerable women figures we encounter in Keats's verse, women who are helplessly trapped and are dependant on an external chivalric force to free them from bondage. In his last letter, Keats sadly referred to his sister in the last sentence, 'my sister—who walks about my imagination like a ghost—she is so like Tom.'[20] Unfortunately Keats was forced to leave for Italy without even bidding farewell to her. Richard Abbey stood as a stumbling block between them.

Another woman figure of major importance in Keats's personal life was Georgiana Augusta Wylie Keats, wife of Keats's brother George Keats. She was the daughter or James Wylie, Adjutant of the Fifeshire Regiment of Fencible Infantry. Born around 1797 or 1798, we have scanty information of her or about her family till she makes her appearance in John Keats's letters on 21 February 1818. Her brothers, Henry and Charles, are first mentioned on 28 June and 14 October respectively, while to her mother Keats addressed the first of his three letters on 6 August 1818.

Keats was extremely fond of Geogiana and he himself admitted that his liking for her gradually increased with time. It was also Georgiana's genuine tact and empathy with Keats's feelings that accounted for the closeness and intimacy. 'I like her better and better,' he told Bailey,

> she is the most disinterested woman I ever know—that is to say she goes beyond degree in it. To see an entirely disinterested Girl quite happy is the most pleasant and extraordinary thing in the world—it depends upon a thousand circumstances—on my word, 'tis extraordinary.'[21]

Against his opinion we may set Dilke's observation, who in 1848 referred to her 'as a pretty, lively, ignorant girl unaccustomed to society.'[22] Georgiana's ultimate marriage with George Keats and their migration to America was disastrous to the health, fortune and happiness of the poet. Keats was deeply aware of the sense of isolation that he had to face following his separation from his brothers. The terrible sense of isolation that engulfed him found adequate expression in his own words:

> ...My love for my Brothers from the early loss of our parents and even for earlier misfortunes has grown into a affection "passing the Love of Women"—I have been ill tempered with them. I have vexed them—but the thought of them has always stifled the impression that any woman might otherwise have made upon me....[23]

Keats conducted a great deal of correspondence with George and Georgiana. In a letter written to her before they set off for their voyage Keats referred to Georgiana as 'my dear sister George.' He composed an acrostic for her in the letter. It was an extension of the same filial affection that Keats had for Fanny that found expression in his letter to Georgiana.

> ...Ha! my dear Sister George. I wish I knew humour you were in that I might accommodate myself to any one of your Amiabilities—Shall it be a Sonnet or a Pun or an Acrostic. A Riddle or a Ballad....[24]

The intial letters of the Acrostic spell out the name of Keats's sister in law. The poem goes like this:

Give me your patience, sister, while I frame
Exact in capitals your golden name,
Or sue the fair Apollo and he will
Rouse from his heavy slumber and instill
Great love in me for thee and poesy.
Imagine not that greatest mastery
And kingdom over all the realms of verse
Nears more to heaven in aught than when we nurse,
And surety give, to love and brotherhood.
Anthropophagi in Othello's mood,
Ulysses stormed and his enchanted belt
Glow with the Muse, but they are never felt
Unbosomed so and so eternal made,
Such tender incense in their laurel shade
To all the regent sisters of the Nine,
As this poor offering to you, sister mine,
Kind sister! Aye, this third name says you are.
Enchanted has it been the Lord knows where.
And may it taste to you like good old wine,
Take you to real happiness and give
Sons, daughters and a home like honeyed hive.[25]

The warmth, love and brotherly feelings Keats had for his sister in law is clearly reflected in the acrostic. The relationship once again reminds us of the filial bond he shared with his own sister Frances Keats. Keats was deeply impressed by the intelligence of Georgiana. She wasn't beautiful in the conventional sense of the term; but her moral virtues, her objectivity, her disinterestedness impressed Keats very much. Till then Keats had traditionally endorsed his faith in the traditional male chauvinistic belief, which in the early nineteenth century was no exception, that 'most women have no character at all—an attitude which does not, however, preclude idealizing them, but arises from it.'[26] Keats was taken aback by the boldness and courage shown by Georgiana. In spite of being just sixteen years of age she did not hesitate to leave her family, friends and comfortable lifestyle in London to settle in America with Keats's brother George. The marriage between George and Georgiana was also the first marriage in the family that Keats observed closely. This marriage, subsequent departure to the United States and their separation from John Keats made Keats more exposed and vulnerable to love. His interaction with Georgiana also contributed a great deal to the maturing of his attitude towards the opposite sex.

Of all women figures in Keats's personal life, the one that is most controversial and enigmatic—at the same time, significant, is that of Fanny Brawne. For the first century following the death of the poet, Fanny Brawne was harshly treated—rather unjustifiably by readers and followers of Keats. The 'Victorian legend' that was cooked up 'was that of a dying poet consumed with unsatisfied love for a heartless flirt.'[27] This false reputation had taken such a firm hold that it became immune to any efforts undertaken to rectify it. Mainly three circumstances contributed greatly to the formation of this Victorian legend.

Firstly, while writing the first biography of John Keats in 1848, Monckton Milnes clearly evaded the presence of Fanny Brawne. He only vaguely referred to a woman whom Keats adored. Secondly, Fanny Brawne served as an easy scapegoat for the guilt ridden minds of the poet's friends circle and even his brother George. They were quite reasonably tormented by the fact that they did not really put in their best during moments of crisis in Keats's life. Ms Brawne turned out to be an easy scapegoat for them, as they desperately tried to convince themselves, that the situation was irretrievably hopeless and all efforts of aid-on their part would have been futile, as Keats was totally obsessed with her during the last days of life. The Dilke family largely provided the 'Victorian storehouse' of information about Keats. So much so, that by the time Sir Charles Dilke, in his preparation to publish his grandfathers papers (1875), was persuaded by his great uncle William Dilke to emphasize that Fanny Brawne was,

> 'not a lady with whom a Poet so sensitive as John Keats would be likely to fall in love. Your grandfather would probably say she made the advances without really caring much for him.'[28]

Even Sir Charles supported this notion of Ms Brawne by quoting her out of context,

> When the first memoir was proposed (a memoir of Keats by Charles Brown), the woman he loved had so little belief in his poetic reputation, that she wrote to Mr. Dilke, "the kindest act would be to let him rest forever in the obscurity to which circumstances have condemned him."[29]

The actual tale behind this is that, while the memoir was being prepared by Brown in Italy, he had written to Fanny seeking her permission to include a letter Keats had written to him about her from Rome without revealing her identity. He also sought permission to include some poems Keats had addressed to her. However, when Fanny received the letter (December 1829) she was facing a new crisis in her life. She had just lost her brother to consumption. Prior to that, a month or so back, she had lost her mother in a fire accident when her garment accidentally caught fire. Inspite of her bereavement, she was perfectly in charge of herself and she gave Charles the permission to go ahead.

Finally, the publication of John Keats's letters to Fanny Brawne in 1878 fuelled the Victorian legend greatly; though seen in the right perspective they should reveal Keats's own inner dilemmas and conflicts.

It was not until the 1920s and 1930s, with the revelation of thirty-one letters Fanny Brawne had written to Keats's sister between September 1820 (when Keats had left for Italy) and June 1824; that the hostile attitudes of critics and readers towards Fanny Brawne started undergoing a change. It was a Boston collector, F. Holland Day who obtained the letters from Keats's sister's family in Spain. He allowed Amy Lowell some access to these letters. These letters did not reveal anything astounding, but they went a long way in presenting Fanny Brawne in a decent perspective. Initially the opinions against her were so strong that Ms. Lowell's attempt to salvage some respectability for her was heavily criticized and dismissed. When Day ultimately passed on the letters to the Keats Museum at Hampstead and consequently when the compilation was published, then it served as a useful reservoir for objective criticism in the following decades. This was especially so for critics who were firmly bent on revealing the truth, inorder to rescue Fanny Brawne from the 'Victorian legend' and present her in the right perspective to readers of Keats.

The early part of Keats's relationship with Fanny Brawne remains obscure largely due to lack of evidence. The elder daughter of Mrs Frances Brawne, a widow since 1810, Fanny was born at Hampstead on 9 August 1800. According to Dilke's assertion, Keats is supposed to have met her for the first time at his residence. He said that Brown,

> …let his house when he and Keats went to Scotland to Mrs. Brawne, a stranger to all of us. As the house adjoined mine in a large garden, we almost necessarily became acquainted. When Brown returned, the Brawnes took another house at the top of Downshire Hill: but we kept up our acquaintance and no doubt Keats, who was daily with me met her soon after his return.[30]

The first meeting in all probability took place in August or September 1818. However, Keats's first mention of Fanny Brawne is in the journal letter that he wrote to George on 16 December 1818:

> …Mrs. Brawne who took Brown's house for the Summer, still resides in Hampstead—she is a very nice woman and her daughter senior is I think beautiful and elegant, graceful silly, fashionable and strange—we have a little tiff now and then and she behaves a little better or I must have sheered off.[31]

As far as Fanny's impression of Keats is concerned, we get it roughly two decades later when she refers to the interesting conversation she had with the poet, except for moments during the conversation when Keats was over concerned about his brother's health.

We get a more detailed account of Fanny Brawne when Keats followed his initial introduction with a more detailed account in a letter dated 18 December 1818.

> …Shall I give you Ms Brawne? She is about my height—with a fine style of countenance of the lengthened sort-she wants sentiment in every feature—she manages to make her hair look well her nostrils are fine-though a little painful-he (r) mouth is bad and good—he (r) Profile is better than her full-face which indeed is not full put (for but) pale and thin without showing any bone-Her shape is very graceful and so are her movements—her Arms are good, her hands badish her feet tolerable—she is not seventeen—but she is ignorant—monstrous in her behaviour flying out in all directions calling, people such names—that I was forced lately to make use of the term Minx—this I think no(t) from any innate vice but from a penchant she has for acting stylishly.[32]

Fanny Brawne, as she appears before us was a vibrant young lady with a remarkable degree of wit. Along with her flamboyant temperament she had the innate potential of application in any form of detailed work—be it studying French or German, or the intricate craftsmanship of tapestry. She meticulously preserved scrapbooks to stay updated with the latest fashionable developments in constumes and dress making. She had a natural flair for foreign languages. Besides learning French and German, she also learnt Italian following her marriage in 1833. She never really had any literary pretensions. Contrary to classical convention, she took a deep interest in Gothic horror stories. We have several instances of her simple, straightforward and unpretentious nature.

Besides this, she had an excellent sartorial sense. She had a great interest in clothes and a remarkable colour sense. She meticulously studied colours and textures of cloth and minutely observed every change in dress designs. She consulted French magazines for latest designs while compiling her scrapbook. She even wrote to Keats's sister advising her about clothes she is expected to wear. A few months before Fanny Keats's twenty first birthday, Fanny Brawne gave her helpful suggestions:

> ...Do not alarm you self about Miss Lancasters appearance. I trust you could cut a better figure than she did. You might feel shy at first (which is not that I know of her failing) but any person of sense who goes out a little can soon get over all that dress manner and carriage are just what she wants a person must be great beauty to look well without them, but they are certainly within the reach of anybody of understanding.[33]

That Keats's relationship with her developed slowly but steadily from the first encounter onwards, there is no doubt—but again we do not have much evidence of its development. The next clear indication that we find is in a rather intense form in the famous love letters commencing from July 1819. The engagement between Keats and Fanny Brawne took place sometime after September 1819. It was made between October 1819, when Keats returned to Hampstead, and January 1820. Fanny Brawne's letters to Fanny Keats confirm this. Although Keats gave a garnet ring to Fanny, yet deep inside he was tense, anxious and despondent. And it was amidst this despondency that tuberculosis was entering its most active stage of destruction.

Some of Keats's intense passionate love letters to Fanny Brawne reveal his surprising frankness in proclamations of love, without any inhibitions whatsoever. Besides the element of frankness, we find a strong undertone of passionate surrender and apprehensive jealousy as well. Here Keats emerges as a passionate possessive lover, and his concern for Fanny quite often mounts to neurotic obsession. The intensity of July reaches its possessive climax in October 1819. Seeing her after a prolonged absence, Keats writes on 13 October:

> ...You have ravish'd me away by a Power I cannot resist: and yet I could resist till I saw you: and even since I have

> seen you I have endeavoured often "to reasons against the reasons of my love." I can do that no more—the pain would be too great—My love is selfish—I cannot breathe without you.[34]

What is strange about Keats's self confessed selfishness and jealousy is the clear absence of the actual third person. The more his sickness aggravated, the more he worried about his love. His insecurity intensified his doubts, fears and uncertainties.

Keats's letters to Fanny can be broadly classified into two groups: firstly, the ten he wrote from July 1819 until he came back to Hampstead in late October, and then those which were written from the following February. Inspite of the scholastic interest directed towards these letters, we would do well to remember that at the time of the exchange of these letters, Keats was only twenty three years old, while Fanny was just nineteen. So whatever passionate sensuous overtones they carry can be accepted and overlooked as a part of routine exchanges between any other persons of similar age.

The later days when Keats was suffering from a string of haemorrhages, he sent a total of twenty two short letters to Fanny. Ravaged by obsession and tuberculosis, these letters carry a constant undertone of belief in the essential fickleness of women. This was, in all probability, an extension of his own childhood experience. As I have pointed earlier, being abandoned by his mother at a tender age, he never really could regain his trust and faith in relationships later in life. One of his lesser known sonnets '*I cry your mercy*' also testifies to the authenticity of such feelings. Whenever alone, the obsessive thoughts of Fanny Brawne accompanied Keats and he constantly brooded over it. As Keats says,

> Upon my soul I have loved you to the extreme. I wish you could know the tenderness with which I continually brood over your different aspects of countenance, action and dress. I see you come down in the morning: I see you meet me at the Window—I see everything over again eternally that I ever have seen.[35]

Wild thoughts tormented the sick poet continually. Time and again, he was ravaged by the worsening plight of tuberculosis. Such torments frequently gave way to despondency. Even the slightest rumour was blown out of proportion by Keats's jealousy. The thought that she had gone to Mrs. Dilke's parties instigated him to imagine his fiancee flirting around in male company.

His obsessive love accompanied him to Italy as well. Before departing for Italy, Keats just could not come to terms with his impending separation from Fanny. During the last days, before his departure to Italy, he undertook painful trips to Hampstead. The old memories haunted him and stirred him with great pain and anguish. Often he sat and sobbed bitterly. The short distance from Well Walk to Wentworth Place contained Keats's most intense associations. The fond memories made it even more difficult for him to accept his premature death. Unaware of the scientific causes of tuberculosis and giving into the conventional thought of the day, even Keats thought that his precarious state was a result of his consuming passion for Fanny. He thought that it was his frustrated desire that literally killed him.

Of the women figures in Keats's personal life, Fanny Brawne is of central importance. Her beauty, stirred up Keats's all too familiar anxiety—that he might be rejected. As to how far this anxiety looms around his women figures in verse in an issue I shall discuss in my subsequent chapters. Fanny as I have pointed out earlier, was rescued from the Victorian legend of being a reckless flirt by her correspondence with Fanny Keats. Her love and genuine concern for Keats is clearly revealed when she writes even long after his death to Keats's sister,

> No one but you can feel with me—all his friends have forgotten him, they have got over the first shock, and that with them is all. They think I have done the same, which I do not wonder at, for I [have] taken care never to trouble them with any feelings of mine, but I can tell you who next to me (I must say next to me) loved him best, that I have not got over it and never shall.[36]

It pained her that she could not be beside Keats's death bed and nurse him. In accordance with Keats's wish she had kept her engagement with him a secret. But no reward was extended to her for her loyalty. After Keats's death she mourned for a considerable span of time, struggling with intermittent spells of her own illness. Incidentally, she continued to wear Keats's ring till the very end of her life. So we clearly see that the anxiety that Keats suffered from as regards his relationship with Fanny Brawne was largely an extension of his own anxiety ridden self-worsened by his severe illness. Fanny herself had very little to do with it. On the contrary, we have several reasons to believe in her integrity and loyalty. Keats's insecurity was indirectly an off shoot of his anxiety and complicated feelings towards the opposite sex—the psychological roots of which can be traced back to his childhood.

So evaluating Keats's relationship with women figures in personal life, we clearly have reasons to believe that his own childhood experience greatly shaped his feelings and attitudes towards the opposite sex. His adolescence, like that of any other teenager, was stormed by fantasies of unfulfilled desire, 'When I was a schoolboy,' he later wrote, 'I thought a fair Woman a pure Goddess, my mind was a soft nest in which some one of them slept though she knew it not.'[37]

Keats's attitude towards woman was often marked by a lack of self confidence. Deprived of a constant sustained flow of maternal affection in childhood, he was hopelessly insecure in his relationships. Coupled with this, he even regarded his own physical appearance as a definite hindrance to his courtship with the opposite sex. The sonnet '*Had I a man's fair form*' is significant, as it reveals Keats's own inhibitions about his short height. Being just over five feet tall he suffered from a lack of confidence in his interaction with women.

However, there were stray occasions when all his prejudices evaporated. One such stray encounter took place in 1814 at Vauxhall celebrations with a nameless young woman. Her fond memories haunted Keats for four years and inspired several sonnets as well. Keats was also equally impressed by Jane Cox—niece of Mrs. Reynolds. Keats met her at a party at the Reynolds house hold. Cox, if we are to believe Keats, was intensely alluring to men. Keats wrote of her,

> She is not a Cleopatra: but she is at least a Charmian. She has a rich eastern looks, she has fine eyes and fine manners. When she comes into a room she makes an impression the same as the Beauty of a Leopardess. She is too fine and too conscious of her Self to repulse any Man who may address her—from habit she thinks that nothing particular.[38]

Cox's sociosexual confidence put Keats at ease. Writing to George and Georgiana in the same letter, Keats said 'I should like her to ruin me, as I should like you to save me.' The comment also reveals Keats's tendency to slot women figures into holy saints and temptresses. He constantly tried to classify the women he saw around him into his own idealized visions. Figures who off and on came in for consideration were women like Ann or Caroline Mathew or Mary Frogley or Isabella Jones and other beauties of Devon.

That Keats had a complex attitude towards the opposite sex is beyond any doubt. It is also beyond doubt that these attitudes were largely shaped by his insecure childhood and adolescence, Knowledge of Keats's personal life in a way helps us to resolve the complexities which plague the women characters we find in his verse. It also helps us to disentangle the psychological strands and trace the deeper roots that account for his diffidence and anxiety in feminine company. Without such knowledge it is extremely difficult to put forward any rational approach or explanation regarding his sexual ambiguity, as highlighted by recent criticism. But first of all it is essential to discuss how these circumstances of his childhood and adolescence combined with other social factors to complicate Keats's own notions about gender and contributed to his ambiguous attitude, as pointed out repeatedly by recent critics. In my next chapter, I shall look at length into this aspect of sexual ambiguity.

NOTES

1. Stephen Coote, *John Keats: A Life* (London: Hodder and Stoughton, 1995), p. 3.
2. Details on Keats's mother were given by John Taylor to Richard Woodhouse in accordance with Richard Abbey's version.

   See Hyder E. Rollins ed.. *The Keats Circle*: *Letters and Papers* 1816-1878. I volume. (Cambridge. MA: Harvard University Press. 1948), pp. 302-9.

   As cited in Walter Jackson Bate, *John Keats* (London: Chatto and Windus. 1979), p. 6 and Coote, *op.cit.*, p. 5.
3. George Keats to Charles Dilke, 12 May 1828.

   See Hyder H. Rollins, ed. *op. cit*, 314 as cited in Coote *op. cit.*, p. 5.
4. Coote, *op. cit.*, p. 5.
5. Coote, *op. cit.*, p. 7.
6. Coote, *op. cit.*, p. 7.
7. Aileen Ward, *John Keats: The Making of a Poet* (1963; rpt Canada: Collins Publishers Toronto, 1986), p. 11.
8. Coote, *op. cit.*, p. 9.
9. Coote, *op. cit.*, p. 14.
10. Ward, *op. cit.*, p. 25.
11. All citations of Keats's poems in this dissertation are from Miriam Allott, ed. *The Poems of John Keats* (1970: corr. rpt. London: Longaman Group Limited. 1980), pp. 526-27.
12. Barbara A. Schapiro, *The Romantic Mother: Narcissistic Patterns in Romantic Poetry* (Baltimore: John Hopkins University Press. 1983), p. ix.
13. Barbara A. Schapiro, *The Romantic Mother: Narcissistic Patterns in Romantic Poetry* (Baltimore: John Hopkins University Press. 1983), p. x.
14. Barbara A. Schapiro, *The Romantic Mother: Narcissistic Patterns in Romantic Poetry* (Baltimore: John Hopkins University Press. 1983) p. x.
15. Ward, *op. cit.*, p. 13.
16. Coote, *op. cit.*, p. 10.
17. Coote, *op. cit.*, p. 186.
18. All extracts from the letters of John Keats are taken from Robert Gittings ed. *Letters of John Keats* (1970; corr. rpt. Oxford: Oxford University Press, 1986), p. 156. Letter written by John Keats to Fanny Keats, 26 October 1818.
19. Miriam Allott, ed. *op. cit.*, p. 361. Written by Keats 3 July 1818 to entertain Fanny Keats.

20. Letter written by Keats to Charles Brown 30 November 1820 Gittings ed. *op. cit.,* p. 399.
21. Letter written by Keats to Charles Brown 30 November 1820 Gittings ed. *op. cit.,* 100. letter written by Keats to Benjamin Bailey. 10 June 1818.
22. Hyder Edward Rollins, ed. *The Keats Circle* 1 (1948: rpt. Cambridge Massachusetts: Harvard University Press. 1965), p. xcvii.
23. Gittings, ed. *op. cit.*, 99. Keats letter to Benjamin Bailey, 10 June 1818.
24. Gittings, ed., *op. cit.*, 105. Keats letter to George and Georgiana Keats, 27-28 June 1818.
25. Allott. ed. *op. cit.*, pp. 355-56.
26. Ward, *op. cit.*, p. 186.
27. Bate, *op. cit.*, p. 421.
28. Rollins, ed. *op. cit.*, p. lii.
29. Bate, *op. cit.* p. 422.
30. Rollins, ed., *op. cit.* p. xlvi.
31. Gittings, ed., *op. cit.*, p. 178. Keats's letter to George and Georgiana Keats 16 December 1818-4 January 1819.
32. Gittings, ed., *op. cit.*, pp. 182-83.
33. Letters of Fanny Brawne to Fanny Keats, ed. F. Edgcumba (1937) p. 92: as cited in Bate. *op. cit.*, p. 428.
34. Gittings, ed. *op. cit.*, pp. 334-35. Keats's letter to Fanny Brawne 13 October 1819.
35. Gittings, ed. *op. cit.*, p. 378, Keats's letter to Fanny Brawne June (?) 1820.
36. Rollins, ed. *op. cit.*, p. Liii.
37. Gittings, ed. *op. cit.*, p. 136. Keats letter to Benjamin Bailey. 18.22 July 1818.
38. Gittings, ed. *op. cit.*, pp. 162-63. Keats letter to George and Georgiana Keats, 14-31 October 1818.

2

Search for a Poetic Identity

IN my earlier chapter I have tried to explore the biographical details that shaped Keats's attitude towards the opposite sex. I also briefly surveyed the women figures in Keats's personal life and how they influenced or revealed his attitudes towards female figures. In this chapter, I intend to look at the way in which Keats's poetic personality as a whole, complicates the issue of gender and how it is in conflict with the prevalent cultural ideology or notions about 'masculinity.' Gender in Keats is a major topic discussion for most recent critics, especially as regards Keatsian Romanticism. Before embarking on this discussion, it is imperative to remember that while one's sexual identity is fixed by anatomy—the traits that constitute 'masculinity' and 'femininity' are greatly cultural constructions. These constructions, according to feminist critics, have been generated by the omnipresent patriarchal biases of human civilization. So very often do we witness the cultural identification of women as merely the negative object or 'other' to man as the defining and overdominant 'subject' who is assumed to represent humanity in general. The traits that we conventionally associate with masculinity are active, dominating, adventurous, rational and creative. In systematic opposition to such qualities, the feminine conventionally represents passivity, acquiescence, timidity, conventionality and being over emotional. Male trespassers from this conventional slots of masculinity were often branded as 'effeminate'—as was the case of Keats. As Anne K. Mellor points in her work '*Romanticism and Gender*,'

> ...Keats subtly complicates the issue of gender and ideology, as others have remarked, either by occupying the position of the woman in life or in discourse, or by blurring the distinction between genders, between masculinity and femininity.[1]

As a male Romantic poet, Keats has often been branded as 'effeminate' by contemporary critics and poets like Byron, Hazlitt, Hunt and others. Keats's unique, unparalleled capacity for feminine empathy that very frequently blurred the line of separation between masculinity and femininity, was the main reason that contributed to this central ambiguity. In his essay, '*On Effeminacy of Character*' (1822) William Hazlitt cites Keats's verse as a primary example of effeminancy. As Hazlitt says,

> ... 'Effeminacy of character arises from a prevalence of the sensibility over the will: or it consists in a want of fortitude...instead of voluntarily embracing pain, or labour, or danger, or death,' lovers of 'exquisite indulgences' want every sensation wound up to the highest pitch of voluptuous refinement, every motion must be grace and elegance: they live in a luxurious, endless dream, or "Die of a rose in aromatic pain"[2]...

John Keats is William Hazlitt's primary example of :

> 'an effeminacy of style, in some degree corresponding to effeminacy of character...one that is all florid, all fine: that cloys by its sweetness, and tries by its sameness.... Every thought must be beautiful *per se*, every expression equally fine.[3]

Even John Keats's friend Leigh Hunt conceded this aspect of inherent effeminacy, especially as regards his poetic style. It was on reading *Hyperion* that he observed,

> ...Something too effeminate and human in the way Apollo receives the exaltation which his wisdom is giving him. He weeps and wonders somewhat too fondly.[4]

Recent critics[5a] have also directed our attention to the original manuscript version that reveals a more feminine original of the ultimate final version in *Hyperion* (III, 124-5).

> Soon wild commotions shook him, and made flush
> All the immortal fairness of his limbs—

Keats's original manuscript reads,

> [Roseate and pained as a ravish'd nymph-]
> Into a hue more roseate than sweet—pain
> Gives to a ravish'd Nymph [new-r] when her warm tears
> Gush luscious with no sob.[5b]

Such an effeminate notion about Apollo is against the norms of not only divine decorum but also that of gender. Such conflicts of gender within masculinity could well be an extension of Keats's own personal life.

Being assigned to the "Cockney school of Poetry" by John Gibson Lockhart in *Blackwood's Edinburgh Magazine* III (August 1818), Keats's stigma of being 'effeminate' was further reinforced. If we look into the dictionary meanings of the word 'Cockney' we clearly understand why Keats was spoilt by 'Cockneyfying.' The several meanings of the word include,

> "A child that sucketh long," a mothers darling: pet, minion: "a child tenderly brought up," hence, a squeamish or effeminate fellow, a "milk sop."
>
> 'A derisive appellation for a townsman, as the type of effeminacy in contrast to the hardier inhabitants of the country.'
>
> one born in the city of London...Always more or less contemptuous or bantering, and particularly used to connote the characteristics in which the born Londoner is supposed to be inferior to other Englishmen:
>
> One of the Cockney school—(adj): 'effeminate, squeamish.' Cockney school: a nickname for a set of 19th cent writers belonging to London, of whom Leigh Hunt was taken as the representative.[6]
>
> (*Oxford English Dictionary* C: 575-6)

Thus, being assigned to Cockney School of Poetry, reinforced the charge of effeminacy against Keats.

Poetry, according to Lockhart, is an exclusive prerogative of the male aristocracy and in dismissing Keats's verse he also ridicules both female and lower class aspirations to penetrate the male aristocratic bastion. He says:

> 'The just celebrity of Robert Burns and Miss Baillie has had the melancholy effect of turning the heads of we know now how many farm-servants and unmarried ladies: our very foot-men compose tragedies, and there is scarcely a superannuated governess in the island and does not leave a roll of lyrics behind her in her band box.[7]

John Lockhart also ridicules Keats, by constantly referring to him by several names such as—'Mr. John,' 'good Johnny Keats,' 'Johnny' the poet of 'prurient and vulgar lines,' 'Mr. Keats....A boy of pretty abilities'[8]—and so on.

Besides Hazlitt, Hunt and Lockhart, Byron too launched a scathing attack on Keats's effeminacy, sexual immaturity, and low class aspirations. Dismissing Keats as belonging to the 'shabby genteel,' or members of working class with 'false claim to the "finery" of respectability.' Byron described 'Johnny Keats' *piss—a bed* Poetry as "a sort of mental masturbation" produced by "frigging of his *Imagination*." Byron is repelled by its 'drivelling idiotism'—'the Onanism of Poetry.'[9]

Both Byron and Lockhart refuse to include Keats in adult male company and consider him seriously as a poet. It was only several decades later, as Susan J. Wolfson points out, that George Gilfillan admired Keats's 'elegant effeminacy'[10] amidst trying circumstances in which he nurtured and struggled with his art. In a condescending tone towards his class origins and poetic aspirations, most poets and critics[11] referred to him as 'Johnny Keats.' As J.R. Mac Gillivray observes, whenever any writer of the nineteenth century referred to Keats as 'Johnny Keats,' they, in fact, implicity affirmed the accusations labelled against Keats by critics like Lockhart and Byron, mainly consisting of 'effeminacy, sexual immaturity, and social inferiority.'[12]

As Keats was described as an adolescent masturbator by Byron, it is essential to take a quick glance at contemporary medical theory, regarding masturbation and what did that really imply and how it strengthened his being branded as effeminate. As Anne Mellor points out in her book, *Romanticism and Gender,* Tissot's extremely popular, *An Essay on Onanism or a Treatise upon the Disorders produced by Masturbation: or the Dangerous Effects of Secret and Excessive Venery* (1758), written originally in Latin but by 1800 translated in Dutch, Italian, French, German and English, argues that by masturbating the person concerned, directed all 'his other erotic energies solely inward,' and indulged in 'self absorption' that often culminated in reversal of sexual roles. The male became effeminate while the female became aggressive.[13] So by categorizing Keats's verse as that of an adolescent masturbator, Byron indirectly re-emphasized the charge of effeminacy against Keats.

What exacerbated Byron's charges was the belief among contemporary publishers that Keats's verse had special qualities of 'general tenderness....delicate taste and refined inclinations....uncontroulable and unlimited sympathy with all kinds of suffering'[14] which would spontaneously appeal to women readers. The epigraph for an article in the 1821 *Pocket Magazine* predicted Keats's exclusive female readership by saying that 'Albion's maidens....Will cherish thy sweet songs!' while Mrs. Sanderford's conduct manual asserted that the 'Gentleness' of Keats's verse 'is, indeed, the talisman of woman;'[15] the *Pocket Magazine* went a step ahead in applying 'this badge to Keats' and making an honorary woman out of him. As Susan J. Wolfson points out in her essay '*Feminising Keats*,' newspapers like '*The Guardian*' condescended to Keats's poems as 'no more than mere entertainments for women.'[16] There is no harm in being marketed to women, but we must keep in view the contemporary attitude toward femininity—which did represent virtues and traits deemed to be inferior to the code of masculinity. Throughout the century, as Wolfson points out, Keats continued to be marketed to publications like *The Young Lady's Book of Elegent Poetry,*

The Ladies' Companion and *The Girl's Second Help to Reading.* These publications compiled,

> passages as referred specifically to the high duties which woman is called up to perform in life, for example, the stanzas from *Eve of St Agnes* quoted by Gilfillan as an instance of the poetry of dress.[17]

The effeminisation of literary values was noted by *Victoria Magazine* in 1870, in an article written by a woman titled '*Keats—The Daintiest of Poets*,' which was headlined. '*Glory and loveliness have passed away.*'[18]

Judgements of Keats's unmanliness were further reaffirmed by Shelley's composition of the elegy *Adonais.* Being greatly influenced by the stories of the reviews, Shelley through his elegy intended to vindicate Keats's dedication to poetry. The elegy too failed to impart a masculine dimension of strength and resilience to the poetic personality. In the sixth stanza of *Adonais* Shelley refers to Keats as—

> The nursling of thy widowhood, who grew,
> Like a pale flower by some sad maiden cherished,
> And fed with true-love tears, instead of dew;
> Most musical of mourners, weep anew!
> Thy extreme hope, the loveliest and the last,
> The bloom, whose petals, nipped before they blew,
> Died on the promise of the fruit, is waste;
> The broken lily lies—the storm is overpast.
>
> [Adonais, Stanza VI]

When Byron came to know from Shelley that 'Young Keats...died lately at Rome from the consequences of breaking a blood—vessel, in paroxysms of despair at the contemptuous attack on his book in the Quarterly,' he just couldn't believe it: 'is it actually true?' was his query in disbelief, 'I did not think criticism had been so killing....in this world of bustle and broil, and especially in the career of writing, a man should calculate upon his powers of resistance before he goes into the arena.'[19] Shelley's 'broken lily' was further mocked by Byron in *Don*

Juan (1823); when he says 'kill'd off by one critique...Poorfellow! His was an untoward fate. T'is strange the mind, that very fiery particle. Should let itself be snuff'd out by an article.'[20]

The myth of Adonais triggered of a spate of reactions. The most inevitable one being the incompatibility of poetry with manliness. The example of Keats's life, especially as glorified in *Adonais,* seemed to be a fragile figure—who was unable to withstand adverse criticism. All these evidences clearly show that in the nineteenth century there was a concentrated effort to standardise codes of conducts for masculinity—which was violated by Keats in his behaviour and literary expression, often to be branded as effeminate. As Thomas Gisborne's manual in 1796 stated, Keats, '"pierced by the shaft" of malicious reviews, was readily translated into this feminine liability.'[21] Another critic Gilfillan asserts that the 'great defect' of Keats was 'want...of a man like constitution,'[22] which incidently Keats even admitted and expressed in his 1816 Valentine poem for Mary Frogley—'*Had I a man's fair form.*' The thoughts of manliness were not only echoed by Victorian critics, but scholars like Carlyle remarked that Dr. Johnson was 'no man to be killed by a review,' while 'the whole of Keats's poetry consists in a weak—eyed maudlin sensibility.'[23] In a rather mocking way Blackwood apologised by saying, 'we are most heartily sorry...had we suspected that young author being so delicately nerved, we should have administered our reproof in a much more lenient shape and style.'[24] In his essay '*On Living to One's Self,*' Hazlitt deals with the issue by saying that the adverse criticism,

> 'proved too much...and stuck like a barbed arrow in his heart. Poor Keats! What was sport to the town, was death to him. Young, sensitive, delicate, he was like "A bud bit by an envious worm. Ere he could spread his sweet leaves to the air. Or dedicate his beauty to the sun"—and unable to endure the miscreant cry and idiot laugh, withdrew to sigh his last breath in foreign climes.'[25]

Hazlitt refers to Keats's death in Rome, and by quoting Romeo's father on his lovesick son, who has virtually lost his manliness in search of love, he gives a new dimension to Keatsian effeminacy. As Susan J. Wolfson rightly points out, 'the effeminacy of Keats's character receives fresh credit for Victorians reading his love letters.'[26] So much so, that even Swinburne makes fun by saying, 'a manful kind of man or even a manly sort of boy, in his love-making or in his suffering, will not howl and snivel after such a lamentable fashion.'[27] So we see that the charge of effeminacy was not only deeply rooted in Keats's own time but it continued even in the Victorian period. It clearly reveals the social attitude, as to how any important personality—in the focus of public attention, was scathingly attacked if he deviated any way from the conventional code of masculinity. The very expression 'Poor Keats' conjured up feelings of compassion and protection. In most cases he was referred to as a 'boy' which indirectly underlined his immaturity and a social misfit for adult company. Even Mrs. Oliphant's account of Keats refers to him as a 'poor young poet...savagely used by the censors of literature.'[28] But the best explanation can be provided from Mrs. Oliphant's essay on Keats for her *Literary History:*

> He turned from the confusions of his own age, which he had neither strength nor inclination to fathom...He was not robust enough for political strife, or to struggle as his contemporaries were doing with noisy questions about the Regent's morals or manners, or the corruptions of the state. It was so much easier and more delightful to escape into the slivery brightness....poetry had become his chief object in life. Those whom life endown more abundantly with other interests may play with their inspiration, feeling towards that divine gift as, according to Byron, men do toward a scarcely stronger passion—
>
> 'Man's love is of man's life a thing apart,
> 'Tis woman's whole existence'
>
> This was the case of Keats in respect to the heavenly gift.... In poetry his was the woman's part.[29]

So from all these evidences we can infer that recurrent references to Keats's effeminacy in literary discourse is not discretionary or deliberate misreading. It indirectly points to the social pressure and the ideological forces that operated around him clearly categorizing the difference between masculinity and femininity. As Susan J. Wolfson points out in her essay *Feminising Keats*,

> ....In his effort to create a poetic identity and win acceptance as a poet, he profoundly internalises and struggles with social and psychological attitudes about gender: at times he is sensitive to tendencies in himself susceptible to interpretation as feminine; at other times, and with more irritation, he imagines the masculine self being feminised or rendered effeminate by women exercising power and authority and at still other times, he projects feminine figures as forces against manly self-possession and its social validator, professional maturity....[30]

That Wolfson is right in pointing out that Keats is sensitive to tendencies within his own self is clearly revealed in Keats's letter to Bailey dated 18 July 1818 where he says,

> ...I am certain I have not a right feeling toward Women-at this moment I am striving to be just to them but I cannot—Is it because they fall so far beneath by Boyish imagination?....When among Men I have no evil thoughts, no malice, no spleen—I feel free to speak or to be silent.... When I am among women I have evil thoughts, malice spleen—I cannot speak or be silent, I am full of suspicions....an obstinate prejudice can seldom be produced but from a gordian complication of feelings, which must take time to unravel and care to keep unravelled—I could say a good deal about this.[31]

It was not that Keats was totally unaware of his effeminacy. Infact, he occasionally enjoyed his straying from the standard code of masculinity as he himself relaxed in 'a sort of temper indolent and supremely careless,'[32] a state he himself categorizes as 'effeminacy.' In the process of doing so he posed a threat to prevalent codes of manliness or masculinity—which people like Lockhart and Byron defended.

> 'The charge is even more specific: Cockney Keats is an unweaned boy—child, unwilling to 'bid farewell' to the joys of early sensual experience at his mother's breast. His vulnerable 'tenderness' enervates the discourse of masculine authority.'...[33]

In *Endymion* and some other poems like *La Belle Dame Sans Merci*—the feminine itself stands for fulfilment. Yet this quest is ridden with anxieties, testifying clearly his own assertion of not having 'a right feeling toward Women.' This looming anxiety points implicitly at Keats's own sexual uncertainty.

Keats's own poetic theory contributes very little to free him from the charge. Keats's famous proclamations about "negative capability" and "poetical character" salvage very little masculine esteem. As Barbara Gelpi and Adrienna Rich[34] point out there is an indirect identification with femininity. Keats resists, quite deliberately, the construction of a masculine self—a self with strong 'ego boundaries...the self as bounded, unitary, complete, and instrumental—the consciousness of self as agent.'[35] As, Keats says—

> ...As to the poetical character itself, (I mean that sort of which, if I am any thing. I am a member: that sort distinguished from the Wordsworthian or egotistical sublime: which is a thing per se and stands alone) it is not itself—it has no self—it is very thing and nothing—It has no character—it enjoys light and shade: it lives in gusto, be if foul or fair, high or low, rich or poor, mean or elevated—It has as much delight in conceiving an lago as an Imogen. What shocks the virtuous philosopher delights the camelion poet....[36]

So clearly we see that Keats's poetic self is something 'inconsistent, unbounded, decented.'[37] Keats himself tries his best to adhere to the ideal poetic character he describes. According to him,

> A poet is the most unpoetical of anything in existence: because he has no Identity—he is continually in for—and filling some other Body—The Sun, the Moon, the Sea and Men and Women who are creatures of impulse are poetical and have about them an unchangeable attribute—the poet has none: no identity—he is certainly the most unpoetical of all God's Creatures.[38]

This process of uniting with the other, being forgetful of the ownself is conventionally associated with femininity. It is the feminine self that forgets and unites with the male counterpart. The femininity of poetic personality is reasserted when Keats compares the creation of poetry to that of the delivery of a child.

> ...Brown has been walking up and down the room a breeding—now at this moment he is being delivered of a couplet—and I dare say will be as well as can be expected—Gracious—he has twins!...[39]

He depicts poetic creation as the maternal act of giving birth in the following extract....

> If you do not see me soon it will be from the humour of writing, which I have had for three days, continuing—I must say to the Muses what the maid says to the Man—"take me while the fit is on me"—Would you like a true Story. "There was a Man and his wife who being to go a long journey on foot, in the course of their travels came to a River which rolled knee deep over the pebbles—In these cases the Man generally pulls off his shoes and stockings and carries the woman over on his Back. This Man did so; and his Wife being pregnant and troubled, as in such cases is very common, with strange longings, took the strangest that ever was heard of—Seeing her Husband's foot, a handsome on [for one] enough, look very clean and tempting in the clear water, on their arrival at [the] other bank she earnestly demand [ed] a bit of it: he being an affectionate fellow and fearing for the comeliness of his child gave her a bit which he cut off with his clasp knife—Not satisfied she asked another morsel—supposing there

> might be twins he gave her a slice more. Not yet contented she craved another Piece, 'You Wretch, cries the Man, would you wish me to kill myself? take that!' Upon which he stabb'd her with the knife, cut her open and found three Children in her Belly two of them very comfortable with their mouth's shut, the third with its eyes and mouth stark staring open, "Who would have thought it" cried the wid [ow]er, and pursued his journey....[40]

These extracts indirectly show that Keats aligned the process of poetic creation with that of female pregnancy and delivery of child. To Keats, 'the mother is the source of life, and poetic myth making can only represent at the level of metaphoric discourse the primal dependence of the child and adult upon its female origin.'[41] However, nowhere else does Keats reveal his own sexual ambiguity and confusion as clearly as in this extract, where he clearly embraces the role of the female when he says:

> It has been an old Comparison for our urging on—the Bee hive—however it seems to me that we should rather be the flower than the Bee—for it is a false notion that more is gained by receiving than giving—no the receiver and the giver are equal in their benefits. The flower, I doubt not, receives a fair guerdon from the Bee—its leaves blush deeper in the next spring—and who shall say between Man and Woman which is the most delighted? Now it is more noble to sit like Jove that [for than] to fly like Mercury—let us not therefore go hurrying about and collecting honey—bee like, buzzing here and there impatiently from a knowledge of what is to arrived at: but let us open our leaves like a flower and be passive and receptive—budding patiently under the eye of Apollo and taking hints from every noble insect that favours us with a visit—sap will be given us for Meat and dew for drink.[42]

Keats here broods on the value of being passive, and receptive like women or traits which are conventionally, traditionally associated with femininity.

Another interesting aspect to observe about gender in the nineteenth century is the preference of modes of poetic expression. Most male Romantic poets expressed themselves in various poetic forms—especially sonnets, odes and romances. However, the ultimate coveted form remained the epic or heroic tragedy for Romantic male poets. Inspired by Milton's *Paradise Lost,* the Romantics tended to regard epic as more 'elevated' form of expression. Even Keats, irrespective of his success with other forms, always cherished the hope of excelling in the epic genre. His attempt to complete a full length epic failed with '*Hyperion,*' which he left incomplete. Such an attitude clearly reveals the amount of heroism expected out of a male Romantic poet writing in early nineteenth century. The epic can be seen as the final test of masculinity. Had Keats been totally indifferent to it, it would have been a different matter. But he responds to it, undertakes the Herculean feat to accomplish it in *Hyperion* and thereby implicitly prove his masculinity. This indirectly shows that he was not content with his success with sonnets, odes and romances—poetic forms in which the popular female poets like Joanna Baillie, Mary Tighe, Hannah Cowley, Mary Robinson and others excelled. Excelling in these lesser, prestigious forms of verse, Keats probably felt stifled being clubbed with the women Romantic poets. So he wanted to break the shackles and prove himself through *Hyperion.*

Thus, we see that there was a tremendous social pressure operating on the poet, to conform to the standards of masculinity imposed by society. Keats himself was not comfortable being branded 'effeminate' and placed in the company of female poets. Though he broods over cherishing traditional feminine traits like passivity and receptivity, like the flower, as in the earlier extract. The poet is not comfortable with it—though it spontaneously arises from within. In all probability, it is the social set up that prevents him from being comfortable. As Margaret Homans observers *in "Keats reading Woman, Woman Reading Keats,"* Keats ultimately enforces 'both the flower and woman into an identification with Jove, the most powerful of the male gods, thus anxiously reclaiming a masculine identity that can resist the seductiveness of the feminine.'....[43] What is even more interesting is Keats's subsequent statement in his letters, where he says, 'it is more noble to sit like Jove that [for than] to fly like Mercury—let us not therefore go, hurrying about and collecting honey bee like, buzzing here and there impatiently.'...[44] This statement completes the alignment of Jove with the flower. The alignment also confirms Keats's association of this traits of passivity with a masculine figure like Jove. Such an association seems strange and contradictory. It puzzles us, especially keeping in view the contemporary norms of masculinity. This indirectly complicates the issue of gender and points at the sexual ambiguity of the poet. He asserts in his letter, 'I will not deceive myself that Man should be equal with Jove—but think himself very well off as a sort of scullion—Mercury or even humble Bee.'[45] This clearly implies that 'he identifies more with boyish busyness than with manly patience.'[46] Here we can clearly take the role of Jove, as the model of masculinity as imposed by nineteenth century society, while deep inside Keats is comfortable being the Mercury. All these discussions again hover around the boundaries of masculinity and femininity.

In social life as well, Keats is precariously aware of his masculine deficiencies. He is too conscious of lacking the masculine prowess as he refers to ownself as

> 'Mister John Keats five feet hight' (Keats Letters, I. 342). 'quite the little Poet' (Keats letters II 61), a 'versifying pet—Lamb' (Keats Letters, II. 116), a 'pet-lamb in a sentimental farce' (*Ode on Indolence*), 'or taken for nothing at all' (Keats letters I. 129).[47]

His entire lament can be summarised in his 1816 Valentine poem for Mary Frogley.

> Had I a man's fair form, then might my sights
> Be echoed swiftly through that ivory shell
> Thine ear, and find thy gentle heart, so well

Would passion arm me for the enterprize.
    But ah! I am no knight whose foeman dies.

(‘*Had I a man’s fair form*’[48], lines 1-5)

It is noteworthy to observe the regret and longing in the last line of the first stanza. We find the traits he longs for in his fragment poem *Calidore*, where he describes the knight as ‘A man of elegance and stature tall.’ (L112).

....
.......................and how the strong of arm
Kept off dismay and terror and alarm
From lovely woman; while brimful of this,
He gave each damsel’s hand so warm a kiss,[49]

[*Calidore a fragment,* 144-47]

That Keats longs to be Calidore, is not a wilful misreading or enforced inference on my part, he himself confesses it in a sonnet, ‘Woman! when I behold thee flippant, Vain.’ (1816) where he says,

Thy winning graces! To be thy defender
    I hotly burn—to be a Calidore,
A very Red Cross Knight, a stout Leander,
    Might I be loved by the like these of yore.

[‘*Woman ! When I behold thee flippant, vain,* lines,’ 11-14][50]

It has been quite justifiably pointed out by a critic that Keats in order

> to express frustrations about writing, he imagines a sexual drama that converts failure to woo the coy muse, poetry, into the cocky confidence of a suitor well versed in courtship ritual: “I know not why Poetry and I have been so distant lately I must make some advances soon or she will cut me entirely.”[51]

In courting the coy muse poetry, Keats also courts the coy ‘wayward girl fame.’ He expresses it in the first two lines of his poem ‘*Fame like a wayward girl will still be coy.*’ (lines 1-2).

> Fame, like a wayward girl, will still be coy
> To those who woo her with too slavish knees,[52]

Keats is aware of inadequacies that make fame elusive, and the charge of 'effeminacy' is one of them. As he says, 'you see what it is to be under six foot and not a lord:... My name with the literary fashionables is vulgar—I am a weaver boy to them.'[53]

What is even more puzzling is Keats's own displeasure at being marketed to female audiences and his own bitter assault on the contemporary women poets. When the legal and literary adviser to Keats's publisher, Richard Woodhouse, was worried that *Eve of St. Agnes* may turn out to be unsuitable for female readership, as no assurances were given about Porphyro's marriage to Madeline, Keats asserted that 'he does not want ladies to read his poetry: that he writes for men.'[54]

He not only discards female readership, he attacks contemporary female poets:

> The world, and especially our England, has, within the last thirty year's been vexed and teased by a set of Devils, whom I detest so much that I almost hunger after an acherontic promotion to a Torturer, purposely for their accommodation: These Devils are a set of Women, who having taken a snack or Luncheon of Literary scraps, set themes—elves up for towers of Babel in Languages. Sapphos in Poetry-Euclids in Geometry—and every thing in nothing. Among such the Name of (Elizabeth) Montague has been preeminent. The thing has made a very uncomfortable impression on me—I had longed for some real feminine Modesty in these things, and was therefore gladdened in the extreme on opening the other day one of Bayley's books—a Book of Poetry written by one beautiful Mrs. Philips, a friend of Jeremy Taylor's and called "the matchless Orinda"—You must have heard of her, and most likely read her Poetry—I wish you have not, that I may have the pleasure of treating you with a few stanzas I do it at a venture—You will not regret reading them once more.[55]

It is interesting to observe that Keats does not like being branded 'effeminate' or being catered to female audiences. He does not stop there, he denounces female poets as well. This indirectly points to the derogatory undertone implied by the nineteenth century cultural construction of 'femininity.' Feminine thus implies all the inferior traits we conventionally associate with it in a patriarchal society, as I have already pointed out in my introduction. The only poetess who impresses is "the matchless Orinda"—a female figure revered for her conventional traits of being 'spiritual, chaste, loving, selfsacrificing, nonrational.'[56] Even age did not wither Keats's hostility to female intellectuals. Writing to his brother and sister in law in 1818 he expresses his disgust.

> Mrs. Tighe and Beattie once delighted me—now I see through them and can find nothing in them—or weakness—and yet how many they still delight! Perhaps a superior being may look upon Shakespeare in the same light—is it possible? No—This same inadequacy is discovered (forgive me little George [ianna] you know I don't mean to put you in the mess) in Women with few exceptions—the Dress Maker, the blue stocking and the most charming sentimentalist differ but in a Slight degree, and are equally smokeable.[57]

He intended 'to upset the drawling of the blue stocking literary world,'[58] through his pursuits in poetry.

So reading Keats in the context of gender clearly reveals several ambiguities. In the process of poetic creation he identified himself both with the male and the female psyche; this sets into play a number of conflicts and contradictions. The fight between the two genders, within his own masculine self complicates the problem of precisely differentiating between the terms 'masculine,' 'feminine,' 'effeminate' or 'feminist.' The fine strand that stands in between empathy and self projection is also an interesting aspect to observe. Keats's own depiction of female figures in verse is more intense, passionate and vibrant as compared to their male counterpart. On the other hand, some of his male figures (like Apollo in *Hyperion*) have been seen occasionally to possess predominant feminine traits—that have time and again embarrassed critics—and even his close associates like Leigh Hunt conceded it. So how should we evaluate this ambivalence in gender? Anne Mellors refers to this process as 'ideological crossdressing' or literary transvestism. The aspect of sexual ambiguity deserves special attention, as even Virginia Woolfe includes Keats in her (all male) canon of 'androgynous' writers and wonders 'whether there are two sexes in the mind corresponding to the two sexes in the body, and whether they also require to be united in order to get complete satisfaction and happiness?'[59] She further goes on to say:

> ....to sketch a plan of the soul so that in each of us two powers preside, one male, one female: and in the man's brain the man predominates over the woman, and in the woman's brain the woman predominates over the man. The normal and comfortable state of being is that when the two live in harmony together, spiritually co-operating. If one is a man, still the woman part of the brain must have effect: and a woman also must have intercourse with the man in her. Coleridge perhaps meant this when he said that great mind is androgynous. It is when this fusion takes place that the mind is fully fertilised and uses all its faculties....[60]

Keats's androgyny, as I have suggested earlier, may be an outcome of his feelings of being an 'outsider' or the 'other' due to his humble social origins and it might have contributed to his feelings of social alienation that he in turn shared with women of contemporary society.

Whatever may be the reasons, the ultimate effect—arising out of gender confusion—is one of fragmentation of Keats's poetic self; which in turn resulted in insecurity, uncertainty, diffidence, contradictions, complexities and conflicts. This aspect of sexual ambiguity, has been the recurrent focus of recent criticism and is crucially important, especially in the context of a re-evaluation of women figures in Keatsian verse. We need to take a fresh glance at these women figures and judge as to how far they are self projections or male projections of gender stereotypes. The process of re-evaluation of Keatsian female figures will also give us an insight into the attitudes and anxieties that beset his poetic psyche in his interaction with women. The subsequent chapters of my thesis will try to explore these issues at length.

NOTES

1. Anne K. Mellor, *Romanticism and Gender* (London & New York: Routledge, 1993) p. 171.
2. William Hazlitt's essay *On Effeminacy of Character in Table* Talk (London & New York: J.M. Dent, Everyman Library, 1959) p. 254: as cited in Mellor *op. cit.,* p. 171 and Susan J. Wolfson's essay, *Feminising Keats* in Peter J. Kitson ed. *New Casebooks: Coleridge Keats and Shalley* (London: Macmillan Press Ltd. 1996), p. 94.

   Hazlitt concludes his essay by saying 'I cannot help thinking that the fault of Mr. Keats's poems was deficiency in masculine energy of style. He had beauty, tenderness, delicacy, in an uncommon degree, but there was a want of strength and substance.'
3. William Hazlitt, *On Effeminacy of Character,* Essay 9, *Table-Talk: or, Original Essays,* 2 Vols (London 1822), I. pp. 204, 202-3, 215: as cited in Wolfson, *op. cit.,* p. 94.
4. James Henry Leigh Hunt, *The Indicator,* 2 (9 August 1820), 352. As cited in Wolfson, *op. cit.,* p. 94.

5(a) Margaret Homans, Karen Swann, Sonia Hofkosh, Marlon Ross, Susan J. Wolfson. Anne K. Mellor, Alan Richardson and others.

(b) Mirian Allott, ed. *The Poems of John Keats* (1970: corr. rpt. London: Longman Group Ltd. 1980) p. 440.

6. As cited in Wolfson's essay, *op. cit.,* p. 95. Mellors, *op. cit.,* p. 172; and in Nicholas Roe's essay *Keats's Lisping Sedition* in Kitson ed. *op. cit.,* pp. 126-27.
7. Lockhart, '*On the Cockney School of Poetry, No. 4,*' *Blackwood's Edinburgh Magazine 3* (August 1818), p. 519. As cited in Wolfson, *op. cit.,* p. 95.
8. Lockhart, '*On the Cockney School of Poetry, No. 4,*' *Blackwood's Edinburgh Magazine 3* (August 1818), pp. 519-24.
9. Lord Byron, *Byron's Letters and Journals.* ed. Leslie A. Marchard (Cambridge, Mass: Harvard University Press 1974-1982) Vol. pp. 200, 225, 217 and *The Works of Lord Byron.* ed. Rowland E. Prothero, London,

1819-1904, *Letters and Journals,* Vol. V, 591. Both. as cited in Mellor, *op. cit.,* p. 173.

10. George Gilfillan, 'John Keats,' in *First and Second Galleries of Literary Portraits* (Edinbugh, 1854), 258. As cited in Wolfson, *op. cit.,* p. 95.
11. Lord Byron, William Hazlitt, John Lockhart, Leigh Hunt etc.
12. J.R. MacGillivray, *Keats: A Bibliography and Reference Guide with an Essay on Keats's Reputation* Toronto, 14, XII). As cited in Wolfson, *op. cit.,* p. 6.
13. Mellor, *op. cit.,* pp. 173-74.
14. 'Remarks on Keats' (J.W. Dalby), *Pocket Magazine of Classic and Polite Literature,* 7 (4 April 1812), p. 333 and p. 335. As cited in Wolfson, *op. cit.,* p. 97.
15. Mrs. John Sanderford, *Women, in Her Social and Domestic Character,* 7th ed. (London, 142), p. 16. As cited in Wolfson, *op. cit.,* p. 97.
16. Lewis M. Schwartz, *Keats Reviewed by His Contemporaries : A Collection of Notices for the years* 16-87 (Metuchen, N.J. 193), 228-32, (it includes the Guardian Review). As cited in Wolfson, *op. cit.,* p. 97.
17. Gilfillan, *op. cit.,* p. 260. As cited on Wolfson, *op. cit.,* p. 97.
18. *Victoria Magazine,* 15 (May 1870), 55-67: As cited in Wolfson, *op. cit.,* p. 97.
19. Lord Byron, Lord Byron: The Complete Poetical Works, ed. Jerome J. Mc Gann. 5 Vols (Oxford, 180-6, Vol. V). and *Byran, Letters and Journals.* VIII 103. As cited in Wolfson, *op. cit.,* p. 98.
20. *Don Juan,* Canto XI, 60. As cited in Wolfson, *op. cit.,* p. 98.
21. Thomas Gisbourme, *An Inquiry into the Duties of the Female Sex* (1796: 7th edn. London, 1806), 34-5. As cited in Wolfson, *op. cit.,* p. 99.
22. Gilfillan, *op. cit.,* pp. 261-2. As cited in Wolfson, *op. cit.,* p. 99.
23. Thomas Carlyle, 'Barus,' Edinburgh Review, 4 (1923): reprinted in Critical and Miscellaneous Essays, I, 277. As cited in Wolfson, *op. cit.,* p. 99.
24. Blackwood's 7 (September 1820), 685 p. 6: As cited in Wolfson, *op. cit.,* p. 99.
25. William Hazlitt, *On Living to One's Self, Table Talk,* I. 229-30. As cited in Wolfson *op. cit.,* p. 99.
26. Woflson, *op. cit.,* p. 99.
27. A.C. Swinburne, '*Keats.*' *The Complete Works on Algerman Charles Swinburne.* ed. Edmund Gosse and Thomas James Wise. 20 Vols (London, 1925-7), XIV, 297. As cited in Wolfson, *op. cit.,* p. 99.

28. Mrs. Oliphant, 'John Keats' pp. 137-38. As cited on Wolfson, *op. cit.*, p. 100.
29. Mrs. Oliphant, 'John Keats' p. 100.
30. Wolfson, *op. cit.*, p. 101.
31. Robert Gittings, ed. *Letters of John Keats* 1970: corr. Rpt. Oxford: Oxford, University Press, 1986 p. 136.
32. Robert Gittings, ed. *Letters of John Keats* 1970: corr. Rpt. Oxford: Oxford University Press, 1986, 228. Keats's letter to George and Georgiana Keats, 19 March, Friday, 1819.
33. Nicholas Roe's essay, *Keats's Lisping Sedition,* in Kitson ed. *op. cit.*, p. 127.
34. Adrienne Rich and Barbara Charlesworth Gelpi, "*Three Conversations*" in *Adrienne Rich's Poetry* ed. Barbara Charlesworth Gelpi and Albert Gelpi (New York: W.W. Norton and Co. 1975) pp. 114-115. As cited in Mollor, *op. cit.*, p. 174.
35. Mellor, *op. cit.*, p. 175.
36. Gittings ed. *op. cit.*, p. 157. Keats's letter to Richard Woodhouse, 27 October 1818.
37. Mellor, *op. cit.*, p. 175.
38. Gittings, ed., *op. cit.*, p. 157.
39. Gittings, ed., *op. cit.*, p. 217. Keats's letter to George and Georgiana Keats 14 Feb-3 May 1819.
40. Gittings, ed., *op. cit.*, pp. 341-42. Keats's letter to James Rice, December 1819.
41. Mellor, *op. cit.*, p. 177.
42. Gittings, ed., *op. cit.*, pp. 66-67. Keats's letter to J.H. Reynolds, 19 February 1818.
43. Margaret Homans, "*Keats Reading Women, Women Reading Keat's*" in *Studies in Romanticism* 29 (1990): pp. 344-45. As cited in Mellor: *op. cit.*, p. 180.
44. Gittings, ed., *op. cit.*, p. 66. Keats's letter to J.H. Reynolds, 19 February 1818.
45. Gittings, ed., *op. cit.*, p. 67.
46. Wolson, *op. cit.*, p. 105.
47. As cited in Wolfson *op. cit.*, p. 105.
48. Allott, ed. *op. cit.*, p. 32 lines 1-5.
49. Allott, ed. *op. cit.*, p. 36, lines 144-47.
50. Allott, ed. *op. cit.*, p. 43, lines 11-14.

51. Wolfson, *op. cit.,* p. 106.
52. Allot, ed. *op. cit.,* p. 512 lines 1-2.
53. Wolfson, *op. cit.,* 106.
54. Wolfson, *op. cit.,* 107.
55. Gittings, ed. *op. cit.,* p. 21. Keats's letter to J.H. Reynolds 21 September 1817.
56. Mellor, *op. cit.,* p. 180.
57. Gittings, ed. *op. cit.* p. 187. Keats's letter to George and Georgiana Keats 16 December 1818-4 January 1819.
58. Gittings, ed. *op. cit.* pp. 276-77. Keats's letter to Benjamin Bailey 14 August 1819.
59. Virginia Woolfe, *A Room of One's Own* (1929: rpt. London & Toronto: The Hogarth Press Ltd., London & Clarke, Irwin & Co. Ltd., Toronto, 1949) 156. Woolfe says: 'One must turn back to Shakespeare then, for Shakespeare was androgynous: and so were Keats and Sterne and Cowper and Lamb and Coleridge.
60. Virginia Woolfe, *A Room of One's Own* (1929: rpt. London & Toronto: The Hogarth Press Ltd., London & Clarke, Irwin & Co. Ltd., Toronto, 1949) p. 147.

3

Bereft of a Voice: Psyche, Madeline and Isabella

IN my previous chapter, I have tried to analyze the gender conflict within Keats's own masculine self. I have tried to examine carefully, the details, pertaining to the concept of his sexual ambiguity, as explored by recent Keatsian scholars. From this chapter onwards, I intend to discuss some of the central female characters depicted by Keats in his verse. I intend to examine these characters in the light of dual strand—as to how far they are self projections of the poet, characters with whom he can empathise and identify and as to how far they reveal Keats's own male attitude towards women. What attitudes do they reveal of a sensitive male poet towards women in early nineteenth century society?—Is the portrayal of women an extension of the poet's own narcissism? Or are these depictions based on gender stereotypes? How far do they reveal Keats's own sexual ambiguity? In this chapter, I intend to discuss three central female figures who traditionally stand as representatives of meek womanhood in Keatsian verse. They are Psyche, Madeline and Isabella.

Keats's *Ode to Psyche* clearly reveals his sexual ambivalence and confusing attitudes. In this ode, as we shall see, Keats takes on the positions of both male and female lover. Written between 21 and 30 April 1819, the *Ode to Psyche* is the first of the Keats's five spring 1819 odes. When copying it out on 30 April in his journal letter of 14 Feb-3 May 1819, he says:

> [the poem] is the first and only one with which I have taken even moderate pains—I have for the most part dash'd of [f] my lines in a hurry—This I have done leisurely—I think it reads the more richly for it and will I hope encourage me to write other thing[s] in even a more peaceable and healthy spirit. You must recollect that Psyche was not embodied as a goddess before the time of Apulieus [Sic] the Platonist who lived after the Augustan age, and consequently the Goddess was never worshipped or sacrificed to with any of the ancient fervour—and perhaps never thought of in the old religion—I am more orthodox than to let a hethan Goddess be so neglected.[1]

The letter reveals two important observations. Firstly, Keats's admission that it is the first and only one with which he has taken 'moderate pains,' and secondly, Keats's genuine concern for the marginalization of the goddess Psyche, whose identity needs to be rescued. The word psyche itself signifies 'soul' and the poet's interest in the subject can be related to the 'vale of soul making' letter, which he wrote almost at the same time as his composition of *Ode to Psyche* on 21 April, 1819.

> ...There may be intelligences or sparks of divinity in millions—but they are not Souls till they acquire identities. Do you not see how necessary a world of Pains and trouble is to school an Intelligence and make it a soul?[2]

I will initiate my discussion on Psyche by focussing on two important aspects which reveal Keats's ambiguous attitudes towards Psyche. The first is how in salvaging the glory of Psyche, Keats tries to assert his own poetic identity; and second one pertains to his own choice of Psyche as a poetic subject.

In the 'vale of soul making' letter Keats emphasizes the importance of 'Pains and trouble,' 'to school an Intelligence and make it a soul.' It is interesting to compare this with Keats's own statement on the *Ode to Psyche,* after composition of which he openly admits of taking 'moderate pains' for the first time. We clearly understand that through the pains of construction of the ode—rather his entire creative process—Keats intends to assert his own poetic identity and establish himself as an immortal poetic soul. As he himself puts it clearly in the letter, which I have already quoted at length, one is not a soul till one acquires identity. For acquiring that identity one has to experience pain. The word Psyche itself signifies the soul, so its identification with poetic soul crying for recognition and identity is rather obvious and clear. As Anne Mellor points out,

> Keats explicitly engenders his own imagination, his soul or psyche, as feminine, following a classical convention that represents both the soul and the muse as female. At the same time, he defines his is possession of that imagination or soul as a kind of rape; his "tuneless numbers" are "By sweet enforcement" wrung and his inspired chorus song will "make a moan/Upon the midnight hours."[3]

Secondly, in his choice of Psyche as a central figure of the ode, Keats once again reaffirms his identification with the goddess indirectly. Keats's own marginalization as a poet, was largely due to hostile criticism, low social origin and several other reasons, which I have already discussed—that aligned him with women—who were also marginalized in contemporary society. In extending his choice as a poetic subject, the woman figure whom Keats chooses is a goddess, who too has been isolated, marginalized and ignored for a long time—till she acquires her identity after the Augustan age. Yet after her embodiment as a goddess, she was not worshipped with ancient zest and was totally neglected. Keats's extension of the choice as a poetic subject—consciously or unconsciously—whatever it may be, reaffirms his own self identification with the goddess. A poet, but not recognized and totally ignored. So the struggle to assert Psyche's identity is in a way, a struggle to assert the identity of the poetic self. Psyche, in that context is a symbol of Keats's own poetic self—a creation of his own narcissism. His interest in Psyche stems not from a wish to salvage glory for a 'valued other' but as an extension of his own self. The Ode is also an acknowledgement, that only through arduous pain and toil one can carve out an identity and be a true 'soul.' The extension of Keats's own narcissism in Psyche reminds us of Anne Mellor's aggressive assertion in her essay '*Gender in Masculine Romanticism,*' where she states clearly that 'instead of embracing the female as a valued other,' the male lover usually effaces her into a narcissistic projection of his own self.[4] Keats's projection of Psyche, as I have suggested evoke similar feelings in our minds.

Keats not only identifies with the goddess but worships the figure as well. The form and nature of worship that we encounter in the last stanza of the ode again indirectly mounts to a cult of self worship—the conscious pains he undertakes to carry out the act of worshipping the divine potential within him—again underlines the aspect of narcissistic self projection. I have already discussed how Keats's personal circumstances greatly contributed to his pathological narcissism in my first chapter.

However, what contributes to the aspect of ambiguity, on the other hand, is Keats's rescue act of the goddess. It is in this rescue act that Keats asserts his masculinity. In the rescue act he is a chivalric, motivated lover trying to salvage honour and glory for a goddess in distress and identity crisis. As he asserts in his letter, 'I am more orthodox than to let a hethan be so neglected.' In a way it is a rescue act of his own cornered poetic self, especially, from the hostile criticism he faced and the adverse social circumstances he encountered in his own life. He is aware of his passive marginalized existence like Psyche—a position which aligns him with the opposite sex—but he is aggressive and active in asserting and carving out an identity for his own self, the identity which he states in his 'vale of soul making' letter. So in a way he aligns himself with femininity and then contradicts himself by asserting his masculinity. He is both the male and the female, both active and passive. It is these contradictions that account for Keats's sexual ambiguity.

The last stanza of the Ode depicts the elaborate preparations of the 'pain' he is ready to undertake to worship Psyche. He is ready to worship her,

> With the wreathed trellis of a working brain,
> With buds, and bells, and stars without a name,
> With all the gardens Fancy e'er could feign,[5]
>
> [*Ode to Psyche*, 60-62]

Keats is ready to exercise his 'working brain' in the process. The toil and elaborate pains promised here, once again remind us of his own resolution to take on pains in life, to suffer and emerge as a true soul in the 'vale of soul making' letter. Keats's internalization of the Psyche here is complete. As Anne Mellor points out,

> ...The poems Keats will write as a result of this ravishment of, or by, his own imagination—the poem calculatedly obscures who is ravishing whom—are figures as "the wreathed trellis of a working brain." The visual image of the spatially radiating, interwoven trellis resembles that of a spider web, the trope of feminine production. And the poem ends with an affirmation of female sexuality, of a vaginal "casement open at night/To let the warm love in!" In this Ode, Keats triumphantly and climactically occupies the positions of both the male and the female lover: he has made to, penetrated, received, and possessed how own Fancy, his own "shadowy thought."[6]

The flow of 'love' through the open casement, at one level, points at Psyche's fulfilment of her dream through union with Cupid. At the metaphorical level we can interpret it as Keats's own craving for the divine grace to be an immortal poetic soul. As Mario L D'Avanzo points out,

> 'In the Ode, Psyche, the imaginative mind, receives her identity from Cupid, the embodiment of passion. Their perfect marriage stands for fulfilment that Keats wished in his poetic life.'

Cupid here is

> 'identified as the embodiment of love or passion, without which the imagination as woman cannot exist. The sexual union of Cupid and Psyche figures the perfect, because

> divine synthesis of emotion and imagination, of heart and head, of sense and soul, a union whose issue is poetry.'[7]

Such an interpretation too reveals Psyche as an object of self projection a creation of narcissism.

In this pursuit of sacred vocation of poetry Keats passively aligns himself with Psyche. By allowing this final fulfilment for Psyche, Keats in a way indirectly affirms a gender stereotype as well. He does not depict Psyche as a 'valued other'—a female figure with autonomy and independence. The last stanza insinuates that the ultimate triumph of Psyche lies in the union—a union not based on embracing the female as a 'valued other,' but a union through extreme self preparation of the female, the fulfilment of which lies solely at the discretion of the whims and fancies of the male lover. So while in rescuing Psyche Keats emerges as a pro-feminist in subjugating her identity at the discretion of Cupid he nullifies the feminist stains he inspires. This in a way contributes to his ambiguous attitude towards femininity.

So we see that the *Ode to Psyche* contributes a great deal to the aspect of sexual ambiguity in Keats. We do not get any definite pattern of behaviour emerging from it, especially in his attitudes regarding the opposite sex. What we get is basically a bundle of contradictions. Yet, amidst these contradictions, certain aspects are very clear. The poet internalizes Psyche and emerges both as a male and a female lover. His internalization also points out that Psyche is an extension or creation of his own narcissism—an element which is predominant throughout the Ode. By rescuing her in a chivalrous way and glorifying her, he emerges as a feminist, but quite confusingly again, after internalizing and rescuing her, disowns her and leaves her totally at the discretion of a male god Cupid for final recognition and triumph. Irrespective of all these confusions and contradictions, it is clear, that he does not represent Psyche as a autonomous, independent 'valued other.' This indirectly reflects a great deal about the nineteenth century male attitude towards the opposite sex—a clan to which Keats himself was hounded and cornered into by critics and social circumstances: and from which he desperately wanted to disentangle himself.

If we examine earlier criticism on Keats's *The Eve of St. Agnes*, we clearly find two distinct critical approaches to the text. This twofold approach gives us two different modes of examining Madeline's character in the poem. As we are evaluating Keatsian attitudes towards femininity, it is imperative to explore these two different strands—for they reveal conflicting attitudes of the male poet in depicting a meek woman figure like Madeline.

Besides this two fold critical approach, which I shall briefly summarize below, there is also the third school of criticism—spearheaded by critics like Douglas Bush, who do not see much inner significance in the text. To Bush for instance, the poem is 'no more than a romantic tapestry of unique richness of colour.' Its special appeal, according to him, lies in 'the incidental and innumerable beauties of descriptive phrase and rhythm' and not in 'the experience of the characters.'[8] The only quality worthy of praise in the poem, according to Bush, is the pictorial and lyrical quality of the verse; so it does not really contribute much to exploration of characters like Madeline.

However, the two distinct approaches I intend to focus on now in order to evaluate Madeline's character and explore Keatsian attitude towards femininity, are totally opposed to one another, and distinct from the viewpoint of critics like Bush. The first approach involves the so called 'metaphysical critics' like ER Wasserman, R.A. Foakes and others who assert that the poem.

> ...Seems to dramatise certain ideas that Keats held a year or two earlier about the nature of the imagination, the relationship between this world and the next, and the progress of an individuals ascent towards spiritualisation.[9]

If we summarize inferences of the so called 'metaphysical critics' about the poem, what we can conclude are firstly, 'the validity of the visionary imagination,'[10] which is justified by the fact that Madeline wakes up to find Porphyro in her bedroom;

secondly, Porphyro's 'quest for Madeline is a sort of spiritual quest or pilgrimage' and his gradual 'upward progression through the castle toward Madeline's chamber represents a spiritual ascent or pilgrimage to heaven's bourne,'[11] and finally, 'the sexual union of the lovers is an enactment of one of those "intensities" of life destined to be repeated, divested of its mutability, in a finer tone in heaven.'[12]

Quite opposed to this metaphysical cult of thought is the more recent school of criticism, with Jack Stillinger as one of its major exponents. Stillinger totally dismisses the metaphysical interpretation of the poem and goes on to add, with slight undertone of humour that

> ...the lovers are consciously intent on experiencing the conditions of immortality—consciously practising for the spiritual repetition of pleasure at an even higher level of intensity [which]—implies, if one reads the critics [metaphysical] correctly, that both Madeline and Porphyro had read Endymion, Keats's letters and the explications of the metaphysical critics.[13]

Stillinger, as he argues in his essay, *The Hoodwinking of Madeline: Scepticism in the in the Eve of St. Agnes (1961),* the poem is nearly a tale of seduction, as far as sequence of events are concerned. He goes beyond that to say that the poem also reveals the scepticism of the poet especially towards dreamers and visionaries. So the two schools of critical thought give two different interpretations of the central protagonist of the narrative: Porphyro. While according to the metaphysical school, Porphyro's pilgrimage is a spiritual quest like that of Endymion: the later school of more recent criticism dismisses him as a seducer, minutely working out 'a stratagem,' to which Madeline is merely a reluctant helpless companion. Since the purpose of this essay is to explore and examine Keatsian attitude towards femininity, I shall try to examine Keats's depiction of Madeline in accordance with both these schools of criticism.

At the beginning of the poem, Madeline is 'hoodwinked with faery fancy' and she puts all her faith in blind superstitions. We find femininity being idealized, as to Porphyro, Madeline appears, 'like a missioned spirit' (L193), 'like a saint' (L222), who 'seemed a splendid angel,' newly drest save wings, for heaven (L223-24). Idealised femininity underlines the traits of chastity and purity in women. The pilgrimage, if we believe the metaphysical critics, is a spiritual one that 'culminates in an act of passion, of the heightened intensity of life, which makes possible a fusion of the sensuous and the spiritual.'[14] Porphyro's passion itself, is raised to a superhuman intensity. In the process of such an earnest endeavour, the mortal Porphyro becomes immortal and unites in love with Madeline, who too by grace of St. Agnes Eve, is in a spiritually heightened state. Madeline dreams and her dream like 'Adam's' turns out to be true, as she awakes to witness the miracle. However, we are uncertain about the feelings that accompany the realisation of the dream. But there is no doubt that her dream turned into reality, be it for better or worse.

Keats's projection of Madeline, in accordance with the metaphysical school of critical thought, is one of idealization. Purity, chastity always hover round her, underlying the iact that these traits form the true essence of femininity. As E.R. Wasserman points out :

> ...Silver and moon light therefore hover about Madeline, the Cynthia of the poem, the eternal form with which human passion must blend. She carries 'a silver taper' (194) which dies in the 'pallied moonshine' of her own chamber (200): she wears a silver cross (221): and before Keats finally described her as a 'splendid angel' (223) he 'tried' 'immortal angle' and 'silvery angel.' She is Porphyro's 'silver shrine' (337), he her beauty's shield, 'heart-shap'd and vermiel dyed' (336).[15]

Keats asserts and reasserts the element of purity and chastity by emphasizing the silver radiance and moonlight and indirectly aligning her to Cynthia—the moon goddess who stands for purity. The union of the two lovers has been given an exalted status. Both attain the exalted spiritual status, which I have already pointed out, that ultimately gives way to passionate celebration of love.

So Keats, in accordance with the metaphysical school of criticism, creates in Madeline a submissive gender stereotype, an embodiment of meek womanhood having more faith in rituals and supernatural grace than in human endeavour. In order to realize her dreams, she has to remain passive, place faith in rituals, superstitions and eagerly wait and dream, till divine grace is manifested upon her in the form of vibrant masculine energy-that ultimately steals into the castle and rescues her. At the metaphorial level if the union of the lovers is seen as a moment of spiritual bliss, then we understand that both the lovers have to undertake a lot of self preparation for the ultimate experience of spiritual bliss in life.

The difference between Porphyro and Madeline is again noteworthy. The former's preparation is more realistic, practical and active as compared with that of the latter. The latter is passively waiting and placing faith in a world of dreams without any active participation in the sequence of events. Such projection of Madeline once again underlines the fact of creation of the meek submissive gender stereotype, totally at the mercy of the male.

What is more interesting to observe is Keats's own alignment of identification with Madeline. As Keats says in his letter, 'The imagination may be compared to Adam's dream he awoke and found it truth.'[16] Madeline once awakened from her sacred vision similarly encounters reality in the form of Porphyro. Keats's perception of himself as a poet thus resembles Madeline's experience. We find that Keats aligns himself with the passivity of the female — to wait and place faith in a world of dreams than of reality, where dreams are synonymous with imagination.

Be it self projection to an extent, or a detached male viewpoint, it is obvious that through Madeline, Keats approves of a submissive meek gender stereotype-totally at the mercy of the male. Masculinity is here a source of redemption for the female. Union with the male is imperative, but what baffles the reader is the male prescription of it as being the sole objective of the life of a female — so much so, that one has to abandon reason and resort to blind superstitions, beliefs and rituals to attain it. The closeted marginalized female is not allowed to exercise her choice in the realistic sense of the term, as a consequence of which, she is left entirely in the hands of fate and relies on the ritual of St. Agnes's Eve, so that a chivalric male comes to her rescue. In this sense, through Madeline Keats does represent or symbolize, a marginalized nineteenth century womanhood vehement protests to which arose through the writings of Mary Wollstonecraft and J.S. Mill. Madeline's helplessness is the helplessness of the nineteenth century female at the mercy of the male. The following lines further emphasise the helplessness and vulnerability—

'Oh, leave me not in this eternal woe,
For if thou diest, my love, I know not where to go.'
[314-15]

If we go by more recent criticism of Jack Stillinger, the projection of femininity that we get is even more distressing. Stillinger argues that the realization of truth after dream is not one of happiness and ecstacy for Madeline, but one of fear, apprehension and uncertainty. As Madeline laments,

'No dream, alas! alas! and woe is mine!
Porphyro will leave me here to fade and pine.
[328-329]

These lines again reaffirm what I have pointed out earlier, that the projection of femininity here is one that is totally dependant on the mercy of the male. According to Stillinger, Madeline is a chaste, innocent and pure maiden who has been deceived and seduced by Porphyro. He portrays Porphyro as a 'peeping Tom and villainous seducer' and this conjures up even a more disturbing situation from a feminist perspective. Madeline's seduction in that sense symbolizes the futility of the values of chastity, purity and innocence that are ingrained in the female psyche from childhood. These virtues are good for their own sake, but in this context, they are used as weapons to subjugate, corner and repress the female. Even when evaluated by a metaphysical yardstick they seem futile, unrealistic, self defeating and mere means or accessories of a patriarchal society to subjugate and seduce the female. The patriarchal society has even woven rituals around them for women to observe and blindly follow. In that context, the Eve of St. Agnes provides an excellent opportunity for seducers like Porphyro, to take advantage of such situations of blind faith and abandonment of reason: to seduce and elope with chaste, innocent and simple maidens like Madeline. Such helpless victims, from their very childhood are taught to place trust in a world of dreams, legends and romance; totally dissociated from reality. While femininity is cornered to a world of dreams, the reality is exclusively a male prerogative—of which people like Porphyro take utmost advantage. Even a critic like Leon Waldoff who tries to defend Porphyro as 'romantic realist' and salvage some glory for him from being branded as a seducer-by critics like Stillinger, cannot deny that Porphyro.

> ...Seizes every opportunity and adapts to every new circumstance. For example, when Angela comes shuffling along, he asks where Madeline is. After she tells him of Madeline's purpose, his imagination flushes his brow, "Sudden a thought came like a full-blown rose...then doth he propose/A stratagem" (II 136-39). When Angela objects, he quickly counters with a promise, threat, and finally "A gentler speech" (I 159) to secure her aid....[17]

It is interesting to observe the difference between Madeline and Porphyro, as Keats puts it, while Porphyro's 'eyes grew brilliant' knowing Madeline's purpose of fasting on St Agnes's Eve from Angela; Madeline, on the other hand, is blissfully 'asleep in lap of legends old!' This once again testifies the cause of the opportunist male seducer, whose eyes sparkle at the slightest opportunity of seducing a female who is painfully trapped in a world of dreams, dissociated from reality—the values of which have been ingrained in her psyche from childhood by a patriarchal society.

To closely follow Keats's words

> But soon his eyes grew brilliant, when she told
> His lady's purpose, and he scarce could brook
> Tears at the thought of those enchantments cold,
> And Madeline asleep in lap of legends old.
>
> [*Eve of St Agnes,* 132-135]

The contrast is to be noted here, femininity here is asleep in rituals, superstitions and dreams. She is bereft of enlightenment as she acts more out of superstitions than out or reason. What somewhat seems to redeem the male attitude is the spiritual dimension associated with the worship of the female. However, the sensual details often tend to over dominate and subjugate the spiritual quest. The description of the feast, for instance, testifies to the passionate appeal that Porphyro intends to make to Madeline. According to Trilling, 'the luxury of food is connected with, and in a sense gives place to the luxury of sexuality.'[18] Stillinger strengthens his arguments of seduction by referring to Keats's acquaintance with Burton's *The Anatomy of Melancholy* and contrasting Porphyro's preparation for a feast with Madeline's fasting on the other hand. As Stillinger points out,

> ...In his copy of *The Anatomy of Melancholy,* opposite a passage in which Burton commends fasting as an excellent means of preparation for devotion, 'by which chast thoughts are ingendred...concupiscence is restrained, vicious...lusts and humours are expelled,' Keats recorded his approval in the marginal comment 'good.' It is for some reason of this sort that Madeline fasts, going 'supperless to bed'[51]. Porphyro's feast seems intended to produce the opposite results, and there is more than a suggestion of pagan sensuality in the strange affair of eastern luxuries that he heaps as if by magic—'with glowing hand' [271]—on the table by the bed.[19]

Irrespective of Porphyro's role as a seducer or a spiritual pilgrim, most critics are unanimous that the poem does explore the central conflict between imagination and reality. Recent criticism opines that the poem reveals Keats's own growing 'scepticism towards dreamers and the visionary imagination.'[20] Madeline represents that scepticism as she seems to end up as an easy prey to the blind faith she places in a world of imagination than of reality. Porphyro is the cause or root of that scepticism. He is representative of the opportunist 'romantic realist' who thrives in a society that throws up ample opportunities for seducing the female. Both Madeline and Prophyro are dreamers, however, while the male has an access to realistic efforts to concretize his dreams the female is denied such access. As Leon Waldoff points out 'if Madeline represents the dreaming imagination and its potential for self deception. Porphyro represents the seizing and adaptive character of the imagination.'[21]

The world 'seizing' deserves special attention which indirectly implies possessing something against its will. While the male has an easy access to 'seize' the object he desires, the female has to accept and resign herself to fate. She is denied access to play an active role to realize her dreams. It does go a long way to reveal the nature of patriarchal society, that does not leave much scope of free will for the female. With core critical attention being directed as to whether Porphyro was a seducer or not, one inference is certain, that Madeline has very little scope to exercise her option. She has very little to choose from, other than unite with Porphyro just after the inaugural rendezvous. We do not get any clear evidence of the union of love, where there is mutual respect, approval and autonomy. The approval of Madeline is an offshoot of her helplessness. She is pathetically dependent on the grace of the opposite sex, even for the slightest form of improvement from the predicament she finds herself in—*i.e.,* being cruelly cornered, suppressed and trapped in a patriarchal society. Irrespective of whether she likes Porphyro or not-that is immaterial—she must accept and stay with him forever. Her reluctance and unhappiness is clear. As she wakes up from dream she utters,

> 'No dream, alas! alas! and woe is mine!
> Porphyro will leave me here to fade and pine.

Cruel! What traitor could thee hither bring?
I curse not, for my heart is lost in thine,
Though thou for sakest a deceived thing—
A dove forlorn and lost with sick, unpruned wing.'

[328-333]

As Stillinger points out,

> 'She will curse not, for her heart is lost in his, or perhaps more accurately, still lost in her romantic idealisation of him. But she is aware that her condition is woeful.'[22]

The world of dreams she is taught to indulge in, is in sharp contrast with the reality. What Madeline speaks about her ownself reveals a lot about the projection of femininity in the narrative. I would like to end my argument by focussing on Madeline's last statement when she refers to her ownself, as 'A dove forlorn and lost with sick, unpruned wing' (l333). The projection of femininity that we get is one of painful isolation and alienation. Her wings of freedom have been clipped by the patriarchal society. If she wants to fly she has to fly on the wings of Porphyro. She is bereft of autonomy and independence of existence.

The meek women figures we encounter in Keats's verse are often victims of the whims and fancies of a patriarchal society. In a larger sense they probably embody the pain, suffering and helplessness of female existence in the nineteenth century society. How women were marginalized and subjugated to patriarchal control is seen only to an extent in the character of Madeline in *The Eve of St. Agnes;* however, it reaches its ruthless extreme in *Isabella.* In *The Eve of St Agnes,* as I have already discussed, there is an element of doubt hovering over Madeline's acceptance of Porphyro. We do not definitely know whether it is an acceptance that stems from a true realization of her dream or an acceptance more out of helplessness and little choice. The sequence of events in the poem, is abruptly truncated with the escape of the two lovers or the elopement of two lovers 'into the storm.' Unlike Madeline, with regard to Isabella, we do not have any doubt whatsoever about the female consent in companionship.

Here we encounter a woman who has consciously exercised her choice in choosing a life partner. The reciprocation of emotions and genuine feelings of love are confirmed as Keats says clearly in Stanza XXI,

> These brethren having found by many signs
> What love Lorenzo for their sister had,
> And how she loved him too, each unconfines.
> ....
>
> [*Isabella,* 161-163]

Her choice of life partner did not conform to the wishes of her brothers. The brothers here symbolize the patriarchal forces operating in a society. The relentless onslaught of patriarchal society thwarts any recognition of feminine free will. Manifested in this poem through the brothers, the oppressive patriarchal forces can go to any extent to prevent a union, in which a woman too has her legitimate share of choice and power. The brothers scheme and devise plans.

> And many a jealous conference had they,
> And many times they bit their lips alone,
> Before they fixed upon a surest way
> To make the youngster for his crime atone.
>
> (*Isabella,* Stanza XXII 169-192)

Keats's depiction of masculinity is one that rings synonymously with cruelty and oppression. In the subsequent lines he says

> And at the last, these men of cruel clay
> Cut Mercy with a sharp knife to the bone,
> For they resolved in some forest dim
> To kill Lorenzo, and there bury him.
>
> (*Isabella,* Stanza XXII 173-176)

The following events, that is, the slaughter of Lorenzo and his secret burial in a forest, further reveal the cruel extent of male domination and indifference towards the feelings and emotions of the female. Isabella's helplessness to her fate embodies the helplessness of femininity, totally at the mercy and domination of the male. The condescending male attitude is more clearly revealed when the brothers resort to lying to their sister. It implies masculine suppression by any means—be it force or tampering of truth.

They told their sister how, with sudden speed,
Lorenzo had ta'en ship for foreign lands,
Because of some great urgency and need
In their affairs, requiring trusty hands.
(*Isabella,* Stanza XXIX, 225-228)

Isabella's grief once again points at the helplessness of the female in the absence of her love. The woman is not the independent 'valued other' but sapped us by the male, so in the absence of that love from the world, she entirely loses her own identity, and wishes to die. As in *The Eve of St. Agnes* the woman figure here too loses her purpose in life in the absence of the male. So much so that she does not intend to stay alive. Isabella starts to 'decay' in Lorenzo's absence and whenever she asked her brothers.

...They spake a tale
Time after time, to quiet her. Their crimes.
(*Isabella,* St XXXIII, 260-61).

A woman is to be quietened with falsity and deceit, and kept away from reality. By means of such falsehood she would be forced to bow before the will of the male and patriarchal order. Amidst such circumstances, for the truth to be revealed what is imperative is divine grace or some sort of intervention from outside. It is then that the vision comes to rescue her from her plight. Prior to the vision her ignorance is painful. The darkness in which she is kept in by her brothers, symbolize the ignorance and deprivation of femininity under patriarchal control. As Keats says,

And she had died in drowsy ignorance,
But for a thing more deadly dark than all.
(*Isabella,* Stanza XXXIV, 265-66)

Keats's projection of nineteenth century male attitude towards femininity has been summed up best by Michael LaGory in his essay '*Wormy Circumstance: Symbolism in Keats's Isabella*' where he says:

> ...Whether the brothers are literally peeping Toms is unimportant. They spy as unsympathetically upon their employees as they do upon the lovers. They represent a selfish and envious state of mind....[23]

A variety of maternal metaphors operate in the poem. Women figures in Keats, are often seen as mother figures—fostering maternal care, affection and protection. As Donald Goellnicht rightly asserts, 'Isabella's frustrated motherhood is....Keats's decorous way of expressing her sexual frustration.'[24] Keats's emphasis on maternal metaphors are recurrent through out the poem. Isabellas' cheek.

> Fell thin as a young mother's who doth seek
> By every lull to cool her infant's pain.
>
> (*Isabella* Stanza V 35-36)

Even the influence of love on Lorenzo is directed to kindle within him, 'the meekness of a child.' Isabella hastens to nurse the basil pot 'as swift, as bird on wing to breast its eggs again,' (1469-470) Lagory points out—

> 'even the allusion used to describe the brothers' gently consciences—
> "Their crimes/Came on them, like a smoke from Hinnom's vale" (261-62) evokes the inhabitants of the valley of the son of Hinnom, who were known for child sacrifices.[25]

Lagory even relates Isabella's 'labour' of grave digging to the ultimate delivery of a child. Lorenzo seems to be resurrected through the basil plant-which Isabella nurtures and cares for as a mother looks after a child. In her *work Imagination-Transformed: The Evolution of the Female character in Keats's Poetry,* Karla Alwes asserts Isabella's gradual transformation from a child to a woman during the process of disinternment.[26] Isabella owes this transformation to the dream vision. Isabella's dream serves as a gateway to the world of experience. The following extract brings out the essence of the poem, in the sense that it reflects Isabella's crucial psychological progression and awareness of reality.

> 'Ha! ha!' said she, 'I knew not this hard life,
> I thought the worst was simple misery.
> I thought some Fate with pleasure or with strife
> Portioned us—happy days, or else to die.
> But there is crime—a brother's bloody knife!
> Sweet spirit, thou hast schooled by infancy.
> I'll visit thee for this and kiss thine eyes,
> And greet thee morn and even in the skies.'
>
> [*Isabella,* Stanza XLII, 329-336]

The dream reveals the truth to Isabella.

> but it also robs Isabella of her remaining sanity, hastens her decline, and ultimately drains the life from her....Deliverance has a price: Prophyro brings Madeline love but takes her into the storm Apollonius brings Lycius truth at the cost of his life.[27]

Through the dream vision and subsequent revelation of truth Isabella gains a deeper vision 'into the heart and nature of Man, of convincing one's nerves that the World is full of Misery and Heartbreak, Pain, Sickness and oppression.'[28]

The growth of basil balances Isabella's decay, as 'she withers like a palm' (447). If the basil represents the resurrection of Lorenzo, then once again it implicitly affirms the growth of a male at the expense of the female. Where the female ceases to be the 'other' and loses itself in the male. We can relate this to the gradual physical and mental decay Margaret undergoes in Wordsworth's *The Ruined Cottage,* in the absence of her husband who is a source of sustenance for both the old Man and the Pedlar who listens to him. The domestic milieu of her home and garden also undergoes gradual decline. In *Isabella* the basil plant, a symbol of masculinity thrives at the expense of Isabella's decay or tears. For Isabella, it is her sole existence as she has lost herself and dissolved in Lorenzo. So much so, that she merges with the vegetative imagery and grows on his grave.

Upon the murderous spot she seemed to grow,
Like to a native lily of the dell—

[*Isabella,* 365-66]

Her 'drooping' (458) image is in sharp contrast to the 'basil green' (458) which drains life out of her. As the basil grows, Isabella withers and decays.

Keats here unconsciously applies the mother—child idiom to the idiom of his lovers and in the process of doing so, he

> reproduces a primary or "pre existing" symbol of human dependency, the double relationship of the fertility bride, source of life, to her son and lover.[29]

The patriarchal forces, as I have pointed earlier, manifested in the form of Isabella's brothers, rob her not only of her love life but her maternal life as well. As a mother cares for her child, Isabella too cared for her basil plant.

For seldom did she go to chapel-shrift,
And seldom felt she any hunger pain.
And when she left, she hurried back, as swift
As bird on wing to breast its eggs again.
And, patient as a hen bird, sat her there
Beside her basil, weeping through her hair.

(*Isabella,* Stanza-LIX, 467-472)

As long she does not conform to male whims and fancies her wishes and desires must perish. And so she dies—a painful, helpless female figure with hope for illusive justice in a world beyond reality—

And so she pined, and so she died forlorn,
Imploring for her basil to the last.

(*Isabella,* Stanza I, XIII 497-498)

So Isabella, like Madeline represents yet another symbol of a meek helpless woman figure, cruelly trapped in a male-dominated society. She is bereft of autonomy, independence and free will.

NOTES

1. Robert Gittings, ed. *Letters of John Keats* (1970: corr, rpt. Oxford: Oxford UP, 1986) p. 253.
2. Gittings, *Letters of John Keats*, p. 250.
3. Anne K. Mellor, *Romanticism & Gender* (London and New York: Routledge. 1993) p. 181.
4. Mellor, *Romanticism*, p. 25.
5. Miriam Allott, ed., *The Poems of John Keats* (1970: corr. rpt. London: Longman Group Limited, 1980) p. 520.
6. Mellor, *op. cit.,* p. 181-182.
7. Mario L. D'Avanzo, *Keats's Metaphors for the Poetic Imagination* (1967: rpt. Durham. NC: Duke University Press, 1971) p. 205.
8. Douglas Bush. *John Keats: Selected Poems and Letters* (Boston. Mass. 1959) xvi. p. 333.

   Also Bush's Keats and His Ideas *in The Major English Romantic Poets: A Symposium in Reappraisal. ed.* Clerence D. Thorp et al (Carbon Dalell. 1957) 239-40. As cited in Jack Stillingers essay. *The Hoodwinking of Madeline: Scepticism in The Eve of St Agnes* in John Spencer Hill ed. *Keats: The Narrative Poems A Casebook* (London and Basingstoke: The MacMillan Press Limited, 1983), p. 144.
9. Stillinger's essay *op. cit.,* p. 145.
10. Stillinger's *op. cit.,* p. 147.
11. Introduction to John Spencer Hill ed., *op. cit.,* p. 18.
12. *Hill, op. cit.,* p. 18.
13. Stillinger, *op. cit.,* p. 148.
14. Ronald A. Sharp, *Keats Skepticism and the Religion of Beauty* (Athens: University of Georgia Press, 1979) p. 45.
15. Earl R. Wasserman, *The Finer Tone: Keats's Major Poems* (1953: rpt. Batlimore: The John Hopkins Press 1960) p. 111.
16. Gittings, ed. *op. cit.,* p. 37. Keats's Letter to Benjamin Bailey 22 November 1817.
17. Leon Waldoff, *Keats and the Silent World of Imaginations* (Urbana Chicago: University of Illinois Press, 1985) p. 73.
18. Lionel Trilling. *The Opposing Self: Nine essays in Criticism* (New York: Harcourt 1955) p. 18 As cited in Waldoff. *op. cit.,* p. 76.
19. Stillinger's essay, *op. cit.,* p. 153.
20. Waldoff, *op. cit.,* p. 80.
21. Waldoff, *op. cit.,* p. 81.

22. Stillinger, *op. cit.,* p. 155.

23. Michael La Gory's essay, *Wormy Circmstance Symbolism in Keats's Isabella in Studies in Romanticism* (Vol. 34, No. 3, Fall 1995. Boston University) p. 326.

24. Donald Goellnicht, *The Poet Physician: Keats and Medical Science* (Pittsburgh: University of Pittsburgh Press, 1984) 195.

25. La Gory, *op. cit.,* p. 329.

26. Karla Alwes, *Imagination Transformed: The Evolution of the Female Character in Keats's Poetry* (Carbondale: Southern Illinois UP. 1993 70. As cited in La Gory's essay *op. cit.,* p. 330.

27. La Gory, *op. cit.,* p. 336.

28. Gittings ed. *op. cit.,* p. 95. Keats's Letter to J.II. Reynolds 3 May 1818.

29. Dorothy Van Ghent, *Keats The Myth of the Hero* (Princeton, New Jersey: Princeton UP, 1983) p. 109.

4

Voices of Discord: La Belle Dame Sans Merci, Lamia and Melancholy

THE most interesting of the fatal figures in Keats is the lady we encounter in *La Belle Dame Sans Merci*. The poem begins with an interlocutor questioning a knight at arms.

> Oh, what can ail thee, knight-at-arms,
> Alone and palely loitering?

The question is repeated in the second stanza as well,

> Oh, what can ail thee, knight-at-arms,
> So haggard and woe-begone?

The knight then goes on to narrate his tale of plight. It is only then we come to know about this mysteriously beautiful woman enticing men and then ruthlessly deserting them. Yet 'the knight cannot tell who the romantic woman was, or where she went, or why, rather, he simply recounts a series of events, which he invites us to assume but does not claim are related.'[1] Another interesting aspect of the narrative has been pointed out by Susan Wolfson, who finds it difficult to separate the voice of the interrogator from that of the knight.

What complicates the task of depicting this so called fatal female character is the scanty evidence within the narrative. The knight's tale evokes more questions from the reader rather than answers. Several questions baffle us: Who is Belle Dame Sans Merci? Why does a ghastly vision of dead men follow the glorious celebration of love? If the lady is without pity, why does she weep and sigh or is it a mere camouflage to deceive the knight?

I shall begin my discussion by focusing on the sources and parallels we have of this female character in the contemporary and earlier texts. Once again these are conjectures based on critical and biographical evidences. We find a similarity between her and Spenser's Phaedria (in *Faerie Queen* II 6). Phaedria hires the knight Cymochiles into her little boat. She decorates herself with flowers and garlands and provides sweet music for him as well. After arriving on an island, she lulls him to sleep with his head on her lap and maroons him on the island. However, unlike Phaedria, La Belle does not lure the knight. It is the knight who initially starts active courtship.

According to Robert Graves, the source of the poem is the folk ballad of *Thomas the Rhymer*. Queen of Elfland takes Thomas to a garden on a milk white steed. There she feeds him with bread and wine, lulls to sleep—like Phaedria on her lap, and finally gives 'the gift of poetic insight.' During the process, Thomas is cautioned that

> 'he might be destined as a Sabbatical sacrifice to hell, going by the road that "lies out over frosty fell"—which Graves identifies with the "cold hill's side" of Keats's poem. The Belle Dame, he says, is the hag Death, one of the triple form of the "White Goddess," and since Keats's brother Tom had died to tuberculosis a few months earlier—she is, he suggests specifically the plague tuberculosis, which leaves "anguish moist and fever dew" on the brow of the sufferer.'[2]

Critics also remind us of 'the beautiful witches Duessa and Acrasia who seduce knights and lull them to unmanning sleep.'[3] The poem may also have been inspired by a painting called '*The Mermaid*' by William Hilton (1786-1839) based on Cunningham's poem, which Keats saw at Sir John Leicester's gallery, a few days before 15th April 1819. The painting presently at the City Art Gallery, Manchester, shows 'the knight of the poem lying dead in the mermaid's lap with a water-lily on his brow.'[4]

La Belle may also have been triggered off by a lot of biographical circumstances. Several critics have spontaneously identified her with Fanny Brawne. In his work *Keats and Shakespeare*, J.M. Murry observes in the poem

> the anguish of an impossible love. La Belle Dame is Fanny Brawne; she is also the beauty of life itself which is claiming, thought Fanny, Keats for its sacrifice and victim.[5]

Robert Graves points out the aspect of consumption, besides of course the reference to 'the elfish Fanny Brawne.'[6] Another biographical evidence has been pointed out by Gittings. He proposed the incident of Amena Bellefila as an important concern for triggering off the female character. It was

> 'in the spring of 1819 Keats discovered that his brother Tom had three years earlier been tricked by some fake love letters sent to him by an old school fellow Charles Wells, and deceived into thinking that a fictitious woman, Amena Bellefila was in love with him.'[7]

This incident along with Tom's premature death, according to Gittings, triggered off the poem. As he says,

> The story of La Belle Dame is, among all its other elements, the story of Keats's dead brother and the cruel deception that first his friends and then life itself, had played upon him—the delivery of his youth to disappointment and Death.[8]

Several critics like Harold G. McCurdy, A. Hyatt Williams have identified La Belle, or rather the inspiration of La Belle to lie in Keats's own mother. Harold G. McCurdy relates the cruelty of La Belle with that of 'the nursing mother who leaves her sleeping child to wake alone and hungry, and who may, besides, drive him harshly away.'[9] In this context we might recall how Keats, himself was abandoned by his own mother, following the death of his father. The knight's anxiety of separation could well be an extension of Keats's own childhood trauma.

So if we consider the biographical details, we find that the Amena Bellefila incident, Keats's mother and finally Fanny Brawne form the biographical background that probably inspired La Belle's character. Having discussed the probable biographical sources and other relevant sources and parallels of origin of the central female figure of the narrative, I now wish to turn to the narrative of the poem and analyse the incidents which would give us a better picture of the depiction of femininity in the text, as well as the male attitude towards the opposite sex.

The Knight, at the beginning of the poem is alone amidst desolate surroundings, when he the encounters the interlocutor. He is 'palely loitering' in a sterile landscape. Nature is bereft of music as 'no birds sing.' The desolation of the first three stanzas is clearly brought out by the poet as he is described as 'a haggard and so woe begone.' The meeting between the knight and the lady took place in the meads or meadows. Keats does not associate her with the traditional haunted forests. In his manuscript, Keats had originally intended the encounter to take place in the 'wilds' but later he changed it to the 'meads.' This clearly reveals, that Keats intended the surroundings not to be suggestive of wilderness. She does not even have the evil traits in her physical appearance, except for the wild look of her eyes. She is untamed and reference to shutting her 'wild eyes' with 'four kisses' implies a softening process. In fact, at the beginning of the narrative, we do not get any evidence whatsoever that the lady had some secret plan or scheme to seduce the knight. On the contrary, it is the knight who is more active in courtship. As Susan Wolfson points out,

> ...Keats allows certain details of the Knight's narrative to suggest that if the lady had a hidden design on him, he, too, was a wielder of designs: no sooner had he met her than he courted her with flowery bindings of his own ('I made a garland for her head. And bracelets too, and fragrant zone'), claimed possession of her ('I set her on my pacing steed'), and, figuratively repeating these motions, translated her words into terms to satisfy his own desire:

'And sure in language strange she said—I love thee true'....[10]

The active initiative taken by the knight is underlined by use of phrases like, 'I met,' 'made a garland for her,' 'I set her on my pacing steed' etc. However, there is a gradual reversal of roles after this, as in stanzas VII and VIII we find it is the lady who gradually gains ascendancy and takes charge of proceedings. We encounter phrases like 'she found,' 'she took me,' 'she lulled me' which clearly suggest a more active role being taken up by the lady. The food showered from heaven in the form of mannadew, suggests that the knight has indeed joined the select band of the blessed. Before entering the elfin grot, she proclaims her love as she says, 'I love thee true.' Even the activities inside the grot reveal very little about the assumed evil nature of the lady. That she weeps and sighs can evoke several responses. Of these responses it cannot be ruled out that she might be full of concern about the fate that might overtake her lover. It may also be that she is mourning her own fate, the trouble she has brought on herself by sanctioning this romance.

In the course of events we come across the dream, which itself has a crucial role to play in separating the lovers. According to Enscoe, the figures responsible for destruction of the knight are the kings and princes who appear in the dream. According to him,

> ...La Belle Dame and her elfin grot are evil, the enchantment of the knight-at-arms is destructive, and their duty is to warn him, to release him from the enchantment, even if it kills him. They are not simply the victims of La Belle Dame: they are her enemies....To them she is *La Belle Dame sans Merci*, and evil, destructive, merciless witch who has trapped the unwary knight and subverted him from his true loyalties. The horrible irony of their warning is that their intrusion destroys the knight as well as the lady: they are the responsible agents for the knight's subsequent desolation and withered state....[11]

The voices we encounter in the dream symbolize the patriarchal forces of the society. These male voices see her as a sort of threat to the knight's commitment to society. As Susan Wolfson points out,

> It is significant that the chorus who identifies the lady as '*La Belle Dame Sans Merci*'—kings, princes, warriors, knight—are representative figures of a patriarchal order defined by quest, battle, conquest, and government, and secured by rejection of the indulgences the Knight associates with her, namely a zone of erotic luxury, sensuality and near infantile pleasure....[12]

The code of masculinity, as endorsed by society requires exceptional standards of discipline and restraint. Femininity here is not only implicitly affirmed as representing something inferior, but also the attitude is condescending. The lady seems to be the target of all offence and attack. She is seen as a temptation which must be overcome for larger accomplishments of life. Femininity here symbolizes everything that prevents a knight from carrying out his disciplined code of duties. The proper masculine code of conduct, as rigidly envisaged by the patriarchal forces, asserts discipline and withdrawal, even if it leads to disastrous consequences. In this context, it is imperative for us to remember, how Keats himself had to face hostile criticism for not rigidly adhering to the nineteenth century code of masculinity, especially in the depiction of male characters in his verse. I have already discussed this at length in my second chapter.

The hostile reaction of the patriarchal figures in the dream gives rise to a legitimate query.

> What both the knight and the warriors of his dream have to gain by defining the belle dame as cold, cruel, lacking in compassion—in modern parlance, a "bitch?"[13]

Feminist critics like Anne K. Mellor offers a clear and categorical answer to this—

> ...What the men gain is clear. Even though the knight is left "Alone and palely loitering" in a wasteland where the

"sedge has withered" and "no birds sing," even though his harsh dream has become his reality and he remains unloved, unloving, even dying, nonetheless he gets to tell the story. The male voice both appropriates and silences the female, we never hear what the belle dame thought or felt. This poem thus becomes, Swann's (Karen Swann's) memorable phrase, a case of "harassing the muse," an unwarranted sexual and verbal assault upon a female whose response is neither listened to nor recorded. This short romance calls our attention to the extreme anxiety Keats felt toward his feminine subject matter, even as he could not then turn away from it.[14]

Critics have identified the lady to represent two dominant concerns. The first being the dissipative potential of love, the second being the aspect of visionary imagination. Critics like Leon Waldoff have asserted that

> 'La Belle, both as a character in the ballad and as an archetypal image in Keats's poetry defines the psychological context from which Keats's skepticism toward the visionary capacity of imagination emerges.'[15]

Yet, as I have pointed out earlier, a great deal of mystery hovers around her. We do not exactly know whether she was real or imagined, except for the fact that she became a haunting image to the knight. From the evidences of the narrative our opinions about her are divided. Before writing "*La Belle Dame*," Keats was preoccupied with reading Burton's *Anatomy of Melancholy*. Incidentally, Keats adds his own comments in the form of a marginal note where Burton discusses love as a combination of 'sacred and profane impulses.'[16] These two impulses are symbolized by two goddesses of love by Burton.

> …One Venus is ancient without a mother, and descended from heaven, whom we call celestial, the younger, begotten of Jupiter and Dione, whom commonly we call Venus….

Burton further adds that

> Ficinus…following Plato, calls these two loves two devils,

> or good and bad angels according to us, which are still hovering about our souls.[17]

Keats's marginal comment states,

> ...from Plato to Wesley have always mingled goatish winnyish lustful love with the abstract adoration of the deity. I do not understand Greek—is the love of God and the Love of women express'd by the same world in Greek? I hope my little mind is wrong—if not I could—Has Plato separated these loves? Ha! I see how they endeavor to divide—but there appears to be a horrid relationship....[18]

In this essay of *La Belle Dame Sans Merci*, Leon Waldoff cites these crucial evidences and backs them up with psycho analytic strands to prove the ambivalent attitude Keats had towards femininity. As Keats himself said about his attitude toward Fanny, in his letter to Bailey, "When I am among Women I have evil thoughts, malice spleen—I cannot speak or be silent—I am full of suspicions."[19]

I have already tried to discuss Keats's complicated attitude towards women in my earlier chapters. His complicated attitude towards women appear in a letter to Fanny (16 July 1819), where he associates her with a belle dame sans merci in Henry Weber's *Tales of the East* (1812) Keats summarizes the tale and explains it to her:

> ...I have been reading lately an oriental tale of a very beautiful color—It is of a city of melancholy men, all made so by this circumstance. Through a series of adventures each one of them by turns reach some gardens of Paradise where they meet with a most enchanting Lady: and just as they are going to embrace her, she bids them shut their eyes—they shut them—and on opening their eyes again find themselves descending to the earth in a magic basket. The remembrance of this Lady and their delights lost beyond all recovery render them melancholy ever after. How I applied this to you, my dear; how I

> palpitated at it: how the certainty that you were in the same world with myself, and though as beautiful, not so talismanic as that lady.[20]

Though we do not have any valid evidence that Keats was acquainted with the tale before writing his ballad, yet it clearly reveals his deep rooted fear of being abandoned and separated from love. *La Belle Dame Sans Merci* stands as an extension of that anxiety. The lady in the poem,

> …dramatizes the separation anxiety as a deep suspicion of woman and as an uncertainty about the relationship of imagination to truth. Both woman and romance, so often identified with each other (as in the sonnet "*On Sitting Down to Read King Lear Once Again*"), are accused of threatening enthralment and psychological devastation. But in fact these dangers are inherent in the poet's desire and the anxiety and suspicions accompanying it.[21]

In this context, one pertinent question which arises in our minds is whether the dream is a kind of representation, 'shifting to the kings and princes the apprehensions and misgivings regarding the lady that consequently arise in the knight's mind?' The lady has often been interpreted as a metaphor for imagination, 'D' Avanzo Mario sees the encounter with the lady and her abandonment symbolizing 'the poet's semicircular arc of imaginative ascent, fulfilment, and decline into the world of reality.'[22] He further, compares the kings and princes of the dream 'as poets who like the knight at arms, have journeyed the path of poetry and have destroyed themselves in searching for its visions.'[23] Newell Ford suggests that the lady not only symbolizes imagination, but something more. According to him she represents an instance of the "Cheating imagination,"[24] but in reality it could well be that

> 'that knight cheats himself, since he may be seeing in the lady what is not there. The sustenance which he accepts from her leads only to starvation and the fairy song which she sings is countered by his waking assertion that "no birds sing." '[25]

In this context, she symbolizes immortality and for any mortal aspiring after her, she may prove to be attainable in brief spells but elusive and fatal in the long run.

In her essay *Harassing the Muse*, Karen Swann asserts 'the woman does not exist' in the poem 'except as a fantasy in which man would find his own completion.'[26] She raises another valid point which again we cannot ignore, she says:

> ...Possibly the knight of "La Belle Dame Sans Merci" is more knowing than he seems, and only pretends innocence. Perhaps he enters into the relationship with the lady in the meads in bad faith, knowing full well he hasn't got a chance with hers, perhaps he, but also the artful poet who exploits without endorsing the plot of seduction, is harassing the Romantic muse, using her to defend literature against other, less thrilling constraints.[27]

Once again we do not have evidence in the narrative to totally refute or accept the interpretation. Another important question which she raises is as regards the object of the knight's quest.

> ...We tend to assume that the knight sincerely wants to capture the lady—that the interruptive warning voices bring home a truth he could not have foreseen. Focusing on his loss, we fail to notice what he gains at the end of the poem—accession to an all male community. Could this community, and not the ideal or even the fatal woman, be the true object of his quest? Is it possible that the knight is using the lady-harassing her—in order to conjure up the warning voices, in order to be interrupted, in order, finally, to become one of the gang, one of the pale kings and princes in whose world "woman" exists only as a delusive fantasy, a memory of a dream?[28]

She further compares the "pale kings and princes" with "shapes of epic greatness" that 'haunted the young aspirant John Keats's dreams and tempted him into harassing the muse.'[29]

All these are the wide ranging critical observations about the lady in the poem. However, at the end of all these discussions, it still becomes difficult to draw any logical conclusion about her character. As I have pointed out earlier, the narrative evokes more questions from the readers than it attempts to answer. Yet on the basis of all critical opinion we can arrive at the following inferences. Firstly, femininity has been idealized in the form of 'La Belle.' Irrespective of whatever she symbolizes, as highlighted by several critics, she is a coveted object of love. The passionate intensity of lovemaking in the poem, reduces her to merely a sexual object. Barring the physical attributes of grace and beauty we do not have any other feminine attribute for which the knight sought after her. There is nothing in the narrative to suggest that she is malevolent or evil, except the 'strange language' and 'wild' look in her eyes. The knight in a way seeks her love by trying to evoke her pity or compassion rather than true merit of his own, for as a 'valued other' exercising her free will, she in all probability abandons him. La Belle in that context symbolizes that kind of female who consciously exercises her choice and discards the knight—for which the patriarchal society accuses her. I have already pointed out that she does not seduce, it is the knight who initiates the process. In all probability through the reality of experience she realizes that the knight is no match for her and so she discards him. In that context the patriarchal forces seem to raise a spontaneous cry denouncing a woman, who has the courage to exercise her free will and discard a male. On the other hand, if we consider the patriarchal voices in the dream as a sort of admonishment for the knight, then the projection or attitude towards femininity that we get is even more condescending and derogatory. In that context, as I have pointed earlier, femininity is seen to be a hindrance, to be overcome for larger accomplishments of life. She stands as a threat to male discipline and must be carefully avoided. She is looked upon as the inferior other, to be shunned for greater success of life, even if that leads to devastation and emotional wreckage.

All said and done, what is most disturbing about the poem is that the feminine perspective is totally ignored in it. We do not get to hear the lady's perspective. She is denied the right to express herself, which clearly reveals how lopsided the scales gender were in nineteenth century society, the reflection of which we find in Keats's poetic discourse. The only words she is allowed to utter in the poem is her proclamation of love, 'I love thee true.' This indirectly affirms that if a female is allowed to ventilate her opinion it has to be in conformity with approval of the male. She cannot speak, rather she is not allowed to speak beyond that. Whether that proclamation is an outcome of the knight's seduction or not we do not know, but surely we cannot rule out that possibility, for we never get any access to her mind later in the poem. The proclamation also serves as an evidence for the knight to malign her glory, we only get to listen to the male version of the tale. The knight goes about telling his story, evoking sympathy from the already over dominant patriarchal forces and ultimately team up with them to wrongly accuse the lady of being a fatal seductress. She might have had legitimate reasons for abandoning the knight as well and does not deserve this harassment. The bulk of the confusions of the poem, probably would have been resolved if we could have had an insight into La Belle's mind. Her silence is not only disturbing but also in the long run it underlines the silence of the nineteenth century female—ruthlessly marginalized in society. Any slight form of assertion of free will, as we see in the case of La Belle leads to ill fame and hostile criticism from the male counterpart.

Like La Belle, a great deal of ambiguity hovers around the next seductress figures Lamia. However, in the former we did not encounter any sort of ambiguity as regards the nature of the lady. In *Lamia*, throughout the narrative we encounter several details that provoke one question after another, with no definite answer whatsoever. Is Lamia good or evil? Is she a goddess or a witch? Is she in reality a serpent or a woman? And so on. Our first view of Lamia is one which Hermes has. Inspite of being a snake, she is beautiful in her own way.

> She was a Gordian shape of dazzling hue,
> Vermilion—spotted, golden, green and blue;

Striped like a zebra, freckled like a pard,
Eyed like a peacock, and all crimson barred;
And full of silver moons, that, as she breathed,
Dissolved, or brighter shone, or interwreathed
Their lustres with the gloomier tapestries (*Lamia*, 1. 47-53)

The physical appearance before her-transformation represents 'a duality, an admixture of beauty and ugliness, and this juxta position of diverse elements reveals a complexity.'[30] After her deal with Hermes she gets transformed. The violent transformation with all its ugliness is described by Keats.

Her mouth foamed, and the grass, therewith besprent,
Withered at dew so sweet and virulent;
Her eyes in torture fixed and anguish drear,
Hot, glazed, and wide, with lid-lashes all sear,
Flashed phosphor and sharp sparks, without one cooling tear.
The colours all inflamed throughout her train,
She writhed about, convulsed with scarlet pain.

(*Lamia*, I, 148-154)

If we closely analyze the lines at the beginning of the poem, we come to know about her real nature. She refers to her own body as a "wreathed tomb" as she says,

'When from this wreathed tomb shall I awake!
When move in a sweet body fit for life,
And love, and pleasure, and the ruddy strife
Of hearts and lips! Ah, miserable me!'

(*Lamia*, I, 38-41)

She clearly seems to be captive,

> …a spirit entombed in a body she wishes to change. The implication is strong the serpent body is something extraneous to the voice speaking real self is the voice—the serpent body holds this self captive.[31]

The narrative suggests some sort of an exile. It also shows that she is acquainted with the pleasures and joys of being human in feminine form, and she desperately pines for that lifestyle. The word 'wreathed' literally refers to the intricate beauty of the snake, on the other hand it also connotes, 'the garland laid on a grave, the mark of a commemorative gesture for a departed soul.'[32] The wreathed tomb where Lamia dwells goes like this,

> So rainbow—sided, touched with miseries,
> She seemed, at once, some penanced ladyelf,
> Some demon's mistress, or the demon's self.
> Upon her crest she wore a wannish fire
> Sprinkled with stars, like Ariadne's tiar;
> Her head was serpent, but ah, bitter sweet!
> As Proserpine still weeps for her Scilian air?
>
> (*Lamia*, I, 54-63)

Enscoe draws our attention to the word 'seemed,' which according to him, underlines the fact that it is only her serpent garb that makes her seem evil, though in reality she is not a demon or a demon's mistress. Modern critics like Bruce Clarke has drawn our attention to the words 'penanced lady elf.' According to him, the word 'elf' usually implies a 'male fairy.' So Keats's use of the term 'lady elf underlines' his sensitivity to the masculine implication of "elf."[33] The following line of the poem also evokes ambiguity and gender confusion :

> Some demon's mistress, or the demon's self
>
> (*Lamia*, I, 55-56)

When Keats implies as to whether she is 'demon's mistress' or 'demon's self,' he implies both masculinity and femininity. The word 'penance' implies hiding one's own self for some sort of shameful act. It is a sacrament involving confession of sin, repentance and submission to penalties imposed and subsequently followed by redemption. It is a voluntary suffering undertaken for atonement. So her reptilian form 'concretizes her shame and self-abasement and signifies an implicit, perpetual apology to the spiritual authority who first authorized her penance.'[34] This 'penanced lady elf' gains her proper desirable gender by bringing together Hermes and the nymph. This clearly reveals the sexual ambiguity of Lamia. It is quite probable that in her serpent form she represents sexual confusion or a hermaphrodite. As Bruce Clarke points out,

> A stealthy Hermes and a jealous Aphrodite are brought together to engender a "penanced lady elf," a hermaphrodite then cast out by a spiritual authority. The complex apologia represented by Lamia's sufferings would bespeak the fate of a feminine soul in a masculine body, or of any psyche inscribed or penned in an inappropriate form through the mortifications of a patriarchal conscience.[35]

This extract involuntarily draws our attention to Keats's own isolation and discomfort with the heavy demands of masculinity and gender stereotypes, as endorsed by the nineteenth century patriarchal society. The 'lady elf' pines to be a woman once more,

> 'I was a woman, let me have once more
> A woman's shape, and charming as before.
>
> (*Lamia*, I, 117-18)

So Lamia, in her serpent state could well be a woman carrying out a penance, on successful completion of which she will probably return to her normal feminine form. The above line also reveals that she is not at all comfortable in her serpent's form and she longs to be in the woman's shape as she was before. It is even more interesting to observe the following lines of the poem, as she says,

> I love a youth of Corinth—Oh, the bliss!
> Give me my woman's form, and place me where he is.
>
> (*Lamia*, I, 119-120)

The words 'my womans form' confirm her identification with femininity. We are here definitely dealing with a woman figure that has been trapped in a serpent's garb, and that account for her ambiguity and confusion. But the bottomline is that she is quintessentially a woman and definitely not a serpent. As Enscoe points out,

> …Lamia is not only a love-goddess, she is the very spirit of human love emerging from the world of primitive passion changing the satyr world through her influence and now with the help of the gods bringing this new concept of love to man.[36]

While Gerald Enscoe sees her as harbinger of the new concept of love, Wasserman sees traits of Cynthia in Lamia, as he refers to the latter as 'Cynthia Serpent,' 'a kind of earthly version of Cynthia,' an embodiment of 'both beauty and ugliness, both goodess and mortal' and only a 'vision of ideal beauty of Lycius.' He clearly states that,

> …she is as much a Cynthia to the mortal Lycius as the nymph is a Cynthia to the immortal Hermes, the difference being that pure beauty is available to the gods, but for man the vision of perfect beauty must be extracted from the ugliness that accompanies it in the world.[37]

There is no evidence in the narrative to suggest that Lamia's 'beauty is treacherous or that her love is false.'[38] Lamia encounters Lycius as he returns being cleansed and purified after offering his prayers to Jove.

> In port Cenchreas, from Egina isle
> Fresh anchored; whither he had been awhile
> To sacrific to Jove, whose temple there
> Waits with high marble doors for blood and incense rare,
> Jove heard his vows, and bettered his desire;
> For by some freakful chance he made retire
> From his companions, and set forth to walk,
> Perhaps grown wearied of their Corinth talk.
>
> (*Lamia*, 1, 225-232)

Does Lamia obtain her release and come to Lycius as a sort of divine manifestation? Or is Lycius rewarded with a sinister female for his prayer and sacrifice to Jove? Does she come to Lycius as a form of redemption or of doom? Of the critics who see her as a form of redemption, Enscoe Gerald seems to be the leading exponent,

> …She is offering to Lycius the same opportunity: for Jove's fulfilment that she had previously offered to Hermes 'in the form of the nymph.' And, as the poem develops, it becomes apparent that Lycius muffs his chance. He is given the opportunity but, unlike Endymion, he falls far short of the complete devotion to the goddess who could guarantee his erotic salvation. And, more importantly, the powers of the world in this poem are immeasurably more effective in combating the erotic spirit.[39]

During the initial stages of the encounter, when Lamia beckons Lycius to look back, Lycius declines,

> He did-not with cold wonder fearingly,
> But Orpheus—like at an Eurydice;
>
> (*Lamia*, I, 247-48)

The reference to Orpheus and Eurydice indirectly foretells the tragedy that is impending. Eurydice having died, her husband Orpheus descended to the nether regions to retrieve her. By virtue of his wonderful harp playing he gained sanction for Eurydice to follow him back to the world above—provided he did not look back at her until they regained daylight. During the course of their return journey, Orpheus could not refrain from looking back at her, as a consequence of which he lost her forever. As Orpheus had lost Eurydice, Lycius too 'loses Lamia and his own life through a different mortal flaw, that of pride.'[40] Both ultimately destroy themselves—a subject to which I shall return later.

The first encounter gradually gives way to proclamations of love. Lamia initially threatens to leave, but all these threats only deepen their bond of love.

> 'Leave thee alone! Look back! Ah, Goddess, see
> Whether my eyes can ever turn from thee!
> For pity do not this sad heart belie—

Even as thou vanishest so I shall die.
Stay! Though a naiad of the rivers, stay!
To thy far wishes will thy streams obey.

....

....

Thy memory will waste me to a shade—
For pity do not melt!

(*Lamia*, I, 257-271)

Lamia stretches her reluctance only to lay a firmer grip on Lycius,

Thou canst not ask me with thee here to roam
Over these hills and vales, where no joy is—
Empty of immortality and bliss!

(*Lamia*, I, 276-279)

As she decides to bid 'adieu,' Lycius grows pale:

......He, sick to lose
The amorous promise of her lone complain,
Swooned, murmuring of love, and pale with pain,
The cruel lady, without any show
Of sorrow for her tender favourite's woe.

(*Lamia*, I, 287-291)

Her cruelty is only a playful game of love, it is intended to intensify her bond of love and she proves it by rejuvenating Lycius with a kiss.

Put her new lips to his, and gave a fresh
The life she had so tangled in her mesh;

(*Lamia*, I, 294-295)

The kiss infuses a lease of new life in Lycius, just as Cynthia's kiss had revived Endymion. While critics like Wasserman assert Lamia to be a 'Serpent Cynthia,' Gerald Enscoe asserts quite contrarily though that 'she is Cynthia with a new name.' He points out,

> ...Cynthia wins the love of Endymion while in her role of goddess, but she is unable to bring this love to full fruition

> until she has also won him in her role as a creature of earth—the India maiden.... Her (Lamia's) transformation from goddess to woman has the same function in this poem as Cynthia's disguise in *Endymion*.[41]

The situation is paralleled in *Lamia*: Lamia wins the love of Lycius while playing the role of goddess, and Lycius believes, at first, that she is a goddess. But like Cynthia, she

> So threw the goddess off, and won his heart
> More pleasantly by playing woman's part,
> With no more awe than what her beauty gave,
> That, while it smote, still guaranteed to save.
>
> (*Lamia*, I, 336-339)

The first part of the poem closes with the apprehension of impending disaster. It is for the first time that Lamia meets Apollonius and both Lamia and Lycius are disturbed. As Lycius asks Lamia:

> 'Why do you shudder, love, so ruefully?
> Why does your tender palm dissolve in dew?'
> 'I'm wearied,' said fair Lamia, 'tell me who
> Is that old man? I cannot bring to mind
> His features, Lycius! Where fore did you blind
> Yourself from his quick eyes?'
>
> (*Lamia*, I, 369-374)

What most critics, tend to overlook is Lycius's reluctance to introduce Lamia to Apollonuis. There is an implicit sense of guilt or some form of awkwardness or apprehension in Lycius that forces him to avoid Apollonius. That indeed sounds very strange for after all. Apollonius, as Lycius admits, is

> ...My trusty guide
> And good instructor; but tonight he seems
> The ghost of folly haunting my sweet dreams.
>
> (*Lamia*, I, 375-77)

Lycius is apprehensive about his encounter with Apollonius, and sees him as a 'ghost of folly' about to 'haunt' his 'sweet dream.' The closing lines of the first part are no less significant, stating that the source of woe and misery for the lovers must come from the 'busy world.'

> And but the flitter-winged verse must tell,
> For truth's sake, what woe afterwards befell,
> 'Iwould humour many a heart to leave them thus,
> Shut from the busy world, of more incredulous.
>
> (*Lamia*, I, 394-97)

The 'busy world' henceforth constantly intrudes and threatens the cocoon of love. The 'thrill of trumpets' carries with it the overture of destruction that is soon to follow. In the final scene we find that Lycius is too keen to display, even flaunt his prized possession to his fellow Corinthians. Leon Waldoff sees this passionate desire of display as an extension of Lycius's own narcissism, for Lamia 'has come to form a significant part of his image of himself, particularly of his new identity as a man.'[42] After dwelling for a short time in the purple lined palace of sweet sin, Lycius is impatient to show off Lamia to the world,

> What mortal hath a prize, that other men
> May be confounded and abashed withal,
> But lets it sometimes pace abroad majestical,
> And triumph, as in thee I should rejoice
> Amid the hoarse alarm of Corinth's voice.
> Let my foes choke, and my friends shout afar,
> While through the thronged streets your bridal car
> Wheels round its dazzling spokes.
>
> (*Lamia*, II, 57-64)

He wants to display Lamia to fan his own male ego. Femininity here is a commodity to display—merely for the satisfaction of the male ego. Waldoff points out,

> ...he wishes to exhibit her beauties in order to enhance his own image.... His desire to display what he calls her "dazzling frame" (II 89) reveals a narcissistic tendency in him, for at the wedding feast her beauty is to be a dazzling symbol of his masculine identity. His love is ultimately a

> form of self-love. When he looks into her eyes, he sees himself "mirror'd small in paradise" (II 47) and he calls her "My silver planet" (II 48) as if she were a planet in orbit around him as a sun calling attention to his brilliance.[43]

Lycius's 'exhibitionistic and narcissistic tendency'[44] underlines Anne Mellor's assertion that the Romantics did not see femininity as a 'valued other' but a narcissistic self projection. Even when Lamia beseeches him 'to change his purpose,' he becomes,

> Perverse, with stronger fancy to reclaim
> Her wild and timid nature to his aim
>
> ....
>
> ....
>
> His passion, cruel grown, took on a hue
> Fierce and sanguineous as't was possible
> In one whose brow had no dark veins to swell.
>
> (*Lamia*, II, 70-77)

Yet she gives into Lycius's plea, being fully aware of her own predicament.

> And knowing surely she could never win
> His foolish heart from its mad pompousness,
> She set herself, high-thoughted, how to dress
> The misery in fit magnificence.
>
> (*Lamia*, II, 113-116)

Lycius's masculine assertion underlines the helplessness and submissiveness of Lamia. As Brian Stone points out,

> ...The cruelty with which Lycius enforce his aim is given Keats's approval in a letter to Taylor: "Women love to be forced to do a thing, by fine fellow-*such as this*." No member of Keats's publishing group thought anything wrong or worth censoring in this part of the poem: which means that the poet is in harmony with the general ideas of the Romantic period. Passionate and tender women are to be 'Subdued' in fulfilment of the 'Fierce and sanguineous' (II 76) desires of the men who love them.

> So, in the poem, Lamia emotionally sloughs off her serpent nature and behaves like a submissive human woman of Keats's imagination.[45]

In the words of Keats,

> She burnt, she loved the tyranny,
> And, all subdued, consented to the hour
> When to the bridal he should lead his paramour.
>
> (*Lamia*, II, 81-83)

So through the action of Lycius, Keats indirectly approves of a standard masculine convention of subduing the female. As to whether he does it for the sake of his publishers and readers or in order to assert his masculinity, is a different question altogether. Waldoff asserts that even Lycius's exhibition of exotic wealth is intended to inflame his male ego and vanity. Waldoff sees his concern for protecting Lamia from the 'penetrating gaze of Apollonius' as a sort of desperate measure to proect his own self, where the woman is just a narcissistic self projection and totally absorbed in the identity of the male. So Lamia's final catastrophic encounter followed by the death of Lycius in a way 'becomes a metaphor for the psychological consequences of denying masculine identity.'[46] Trilling compares the two worlds of love, 'one of elfin grot created by La Belle and the other of the Place' created by Lamia, and asserts that both these scenes of 'erotic pleasure' ultimately 'leads to devastation, of an erotic fulfilment which implies castration.'[47] Trilling also points out that Keats not only advocates or depicts a world of pleasure and sensations in his verse, he also extends his skepticism towards it. In *Lamia*, Apollonius can be seen as that agent of skepticism.

In the final encounter Lycius desperately tries to protect Lamia from Apollonius, Apollonius confronts Lamia in the banquet hall, following which Lamia being attacked as a 'serpent!' disappears and Lycius dies. As Leon Waldoff points out in psychoanalytic terms,

> ...(Apollonius's) attack on and the disappearance of the prime symbol of the hero's masculine identity results in

> his death suggesting both castration and phychological devastation.................
>
> .... Central to the idea of tragedy in this poem is the fact that Lycius's identity and life have become fatefully intertwined with the illusion of a feminine ideal behind which hides, in the nature of a serpent, the image of a phallic woman. Apollonius's repetition of the charge that she is a serpent is the climax of a recognition scene exposing one of the most fearful images associated with woman, an image symbolizing to the observing Lycius his powerlessness. In the final scene, Lamia's kinship—with the fearful gorgons of myth and literature is silently but forcefully evoked and Lycius's death is related to the fate of those who have looked on Medusa's head...[48]

So the two major reasons, behind Lycius's death following Lamia's disappearance, according to Waldoff are: firstly, 'her disappearance and his recognition of her serpent's nature,' gives 'a fatal wound to his male narcissism, his identity as a man,' secondly, it is the culmination of what Waldoff calls, 'castration anxiety,' that is Keats's

> deep suspicion that a woman, by her inconstant, abandoning or deceptive behaviour or perhaps by some unnatural power that she possesses could unman the poet and destroy him.[49]

Besides Waldoff's psychological insight, most other critics have tended to argue on conventional lines. To them Lamia is evil, malevolent, ambiguous and sinister; Lycius being naïve, innocent and vulnerable, and Apollonius the firm, resolute philosopher. According to Clarence D. Thorpe, Lamia is only 'apparently beautiful,' representing 'mere sensuous passion, feeling without knowledge, empty dreams.' He sees Apollonius's cold philosophy as Keats's criticism of his own self, the intellect in its awakened state, as he states 'the youngster who loves so unwisely also dies—though in its place is born a stronger, firmer soul.'[50] H.W. Garrod[51] sees her as evil and identifies her with a snake, R.D. Havens sees Lamia as 'a snake, a deceiver, with powers of dubious origin.'[52] Newell Ford sees her as an embodiment of sensual beauty, 'however entrancing and highly to be treasured is only "aery nothing."'[53] Sidney Colvin points out her fatality and poses several queries questioning the credibility of the seriousness of the verse. Referring to the sequence of events of Lamia's disappearance, Lycius's death and Apollonius's wisdom; Colvin asks,

> …Are these things a bitter parable of universal application, meaning that all love-joys are but deception and at the touch of wisdom and experience they melt away? Why are we asked to take sides with the enchantress ignoring everything about her except her charm, and against the sage?…
>
> …Is there not in all this a slackening of imaginative and intellectual grasp? It is a cheap and unilluminating repetition of a rather superficial idea…not fit to stand in serious poetry.[54]

Several critics have asserted Keats's own identity with Lycius. In his work *Keats and Shakespeare*, Murry observed that….

> …Lamia is imaginative autobiography, and of the most exact and faithful kind. Keats is Lycuis, Fanny Brawne is Lamia, and Apollonius is Charles Brown the realist, trying to break Fanny's spell over Keats by insisting upon her as the female animal….[55]

Bush, however, cautions that Lycius stands as 'a projection of only one part, and not the strongest part of Keats himself.'[56]

Lycius's death at the disappearance of Lamia does not come as a surprise for us. We have already seen recurrent examples in Keats where sudden absence of the 'feminine ideal' causes intense depression. The separation in La Belle, which I have already discussed, is one such example. Asked to choose between death and separation, Keats prefers the former in his sonnet "*Bright Star.*" At the end of *Endymion*, Endymion wishes to have a last glimpse of the Indian maiden and only then die. In

Lamia too, in the first part, when Lamia intends to leave Lycius, he too wishes to die.

Psychoanalytic critics have referred to Lamia as unnatural and related her serpent nature to that of a 'phallic woman.'

> …an imaginary figure encountered in dreams, myths, art and literatures. One thinks especially of Medusa and Lilith but also of Circe, Acrasia and other who are associated with a primordial and potentially fatal fear in the observer. From a psychoanalytic point of view, the figure of a phallie woman is thought to derive from an infantile image of the preoedipal mother as possessing a penis and threatening a variety of arbitrary punishments, including death….[57]
>
> (Freud "*On the Sexual Theories of Children*" *Standard Edition* IX 216-17).

So, besides the reason of desertion of the feminine ideal to which Lycius was fatally attached, it could well be that Lamia's revelation as a 'phallic woman' was too brutal an attack on his own narcissism which was too much for Lycius to digest—that leads to his psychological ruin.

The word 'Lamiae' in *Lempriere's Classical Dictionary* conveys details which might explain her reptilian existence. It refers to 'Lamiae' as African monsters having face and breast of woman, which the remaining portion of the body like that of a serpent. They tempted strangers in order to devour them. There is also a fable which states that Jupiter's lust for beautiful Lamia evoked the jealousy of Juno. Juno out of jealousy deformed Jupiter and killed the children of Lamia following which Lamia became deranged and consumed all children that came her way. Lamia's serpent origin, gradual transformation and final catastrophe owes its origin probably *to Lempriere's Classical Dictionary* with which Keats was well acquainted. Clarke points out, 'Jupiter's destructive dalliance here is of a piece with Olympian patriarchal prerogatives, one paradigm of which is the parable of the "ever smitten" Hermes in conquest of nymph.'[58]

In the final encounter between Lamia and Apollonius one element is definite that no matter, how much of a 'trusty guide' and 'good instructor' Apollonius is, his entry in the scene is uninvited and unwarranted. He virtually imposes himself upon the life of his disciple. As Lycius exclaims:

> 'Shut, shut those juggling eyes, thou ruthless man!
> Then them aside, wretch! Or the righteous ban
> Of all the Gods, whose dreadful images
> Here represent their shadowy presences,
> May pierce them on the sudden with the thorn
> Of painful blindness; leaving thee forlorn,
> In trembling dotage to the feeblest fright
> Of conscience, for their long offended might,
> For all thine impious proud-heart sophistries,
> Unlawful magic, and enticing lies.
>
> (*Lamia*, II, Lines 277-286)

The reason behind Apollonius's attack against Lamia as a serpent is not sustained by the narrative. There may be a great deal of scheming but there is nothing in the narrative to confirm that she is wholly malevolent and evil. What is interesting to observe is that while Apollonius launches his attack on Lamia, Lycius's attack is directed at his guide and mentor. His philosophy is referred to by Lycius as 'impious, proud heart sophistries,' 'enticing lies,' 'unlawful magic.' These terms are precisely the ones that Apollonius would probably apply to Lamia. Lycius virtually denounces him.

> ...that gray-beard wretch!
> Mark how, possessed, his lashless eyelids stretch
> Around his demon eyes! Corinthians, see!
> My sweet bride withers at their potency....
>
> (*Lamia*, II, 287-290)

In the first part, Lamia herself was described as a demon, here it is reversed as Apollonius is described in demonic terms. His lashless eyelids suggest his affinity with a serpent. As Clarke points out,

> ...Some notion of "philosophic acumen and virtue" is not sufficient to account for Apollonius's 'recognition and the virulence of his power. Apollonius's humanity is at least as questionable as Lamia's daemonic status. The two are rather, if not equal, at least qualitatively comparable players in an intrigue that has left the all-too-human Lycius far behind. Apollonius knows Lamia: Shall we say, it takes a thief to know one?...[59]

It is Apollonius's over possessive nature that disallows the union of Lamia and Lycius. His over possessive dictatorial nature does not even allow Lycius to exercise his free will and freedom of choice. He encroaches upon Lycius's freedom as if it is his supreme prerogative. While the majority of traditional critics tend to defend Apollonius's act; Gerald Enscoe, one of the few exceptions, asks a legitimate question as regards the sequence of events, that is, the destruction of Lamia by Apollonius and the subsequent death of Lycius. He affirms,

> ...If the influence of Lamia over Lycius is evil, to be removed like a cancerous growth, we ought to hope for a healthier patient after surgery. But an operation in which the patient dies can hardly be called a success....[60]

Apollonius's obsessive, over possessive nature as regards Lycius is in all probability a definite hindrance to the growth of Lycius's personality. He even denies the minimum freedom to a mature adult in making his choice of a life partner. His egocentricity, imposing, possessive and interfering nature is clearly revealed in the following lines,

> 'Fool!' said the sophist, in an under-tone
> Gruff with contempt, which a death-nighing moan
> From Lycius answered, as heart-struck and lost,
> He sank supine beside the aching ghost.
> 'Fool! Fool!' repeated he, while his eyes still
> Relented not, nor moved: 'From every ill
> Of life have I preserved thee to this day,
> And shall I see thee made a serpent's prey?'
>
> (*Lamia*, II, 291-298)

These lines carry two implications. Firstly, his failure as an instructor and mentor which has failed to impart any defence mechanism in Lycius to enable him to abstain from all evil. It also implies his ruthlessness, that he would not even abstain from rectifying his disciple even if it goes to the extent of destroying him totally. The bottomline is that Lycius has to adhere to his will or else he must perish. For a man of wisdom of Apollonius's repute what would have been more desirable is a gentle reprimand to Lycius. The rest should have been left to his prudence. After all his words of wisdom had already contributed to shaping the character of Lycius.

Apollonius here represents patriarchal forces that oppress society indirectly. Firstly, it straight way disapproves of a sexually conscious woman—who independently exercises her freedom of choice and actively pursues it towards fulfilment; and secondly, it also disapproves of a male, who reciprocates or gives sanction to such female love. If that male does not listen to the patriarchal voices of authority, it goes to the extent of destroying both the male and female without any remorse whatsoever. We are once again reminded of the gross use of force by patriarchal forces to serve its end. We have seen its manifestation before in *Isabella*, through Isabella's brothers. Here in *Lamia*, patriarchal authority comes garbed in the form of an old philosopher who forcibly intervenes to crush any form of assertion of free will by an woman. The tussle between Apollonius and Lycius is the tussle as regards endorsement or approval of femininity. While Lycius is more liberal in accepting Lamia, Apollonius is rigid, firm and resolved. The sexual symbolism here is also very strong, along with the patriarchal assertion. As Clarke points out,

> ...Apollonius is the anti-Dionysius, the patriarchal superego, the ascetic idealist whose gaze derives its withering potency from the negativity of his sublimations, that is, from his drawing up of eros from the phallus to the eye, "like a sharp spear...keen, cruel, perceant, stinging."[61]

Apollonius's behaviour aligns him with the knights and warriors we encounter in *La Belle Dame Sans Merci* who label the lady a merciless cruel character. Both apply evil names to the feminine characters, and try to malign their reputations, after which they have to abruptly disappear from society.

The patriarchal forces may win, but they have to pay a heavy price for their victory. As Gerald Enscoe points out,

> …Man without the "elfin grot" or the "pleasure palace" is left like the dying "knight—at-arms" on the "cold hillside," "alone and palely loitering," or like Lycius, bereft of life itself…[62]

In *Lamia*, Keats clearly shows the failure of a woman who consciously tries to exercise her free will. She may be a seducer, but her relationship with Lycius is based on mutual consent and love. If any force can stand as a source of legitimate hindrance to the relationship it is either Lycius or Lamia's free will and not any external agent. Even in the role of a seductress she preserves the legitimate prerogative to pursue her obsession with love. Yet what does her disappearance signify? Does it signify her return to original serpent state? We do not know, we can only conjecture. What haunts us is the question whether femininity would ever emerge as a free, independent and autonomous entity within her own limitations and be regarded as a 'valued other.' We find a similar echo in Clarke's words when he asks,

> …Will Lamia ever have her own being, independent of the fantasies and prohibitions of some other agent? The dilemma and as yet unresolved penance of the feminine within a patriarchal culture is to be inescapably contaminated with male fantasies and prohibitions. "I was a woman once" means "I was once unsubmitted to patriarchal mortifications." That Keats could imagine for Lamia no ultimate escape from Apollonious's tyranny dramatizes the tempered bewilderment of a poet who knew he needed to make his peace with the spirit of the fathers but could foresee only death as the outcome of that peace…[63]

In that context again, Clarke indirectly hits out at Keats's sexual ambiguity, where he indirectly aligns himself with the female and raises his voice of protest against the patriarchal forces of society that demand exceptional standards of masculinity from him. In terms of social conventions he often falls short of such expectations. So through *Lamia* he clearly intended to launch a scathing attack against the over dominant patriarchal forces of society.

There is a strong undertone of fatality associated with Keats's characterization of Melancholy in his *Ode on Melancholy*. Melancholy was Keats's life long companion ever since his childhood. It has been a recurrent backdrop of most of his odes and letters. As Robert Gittings points out in his biography,

> …his own innate tendency to melancholy. Suspicion, with the profound and sudden disquiet which his friends noticed, and which he had himself made so many attempts to resolve in poetry and in thought….[64]

In May 1817, when Keats wrote to Haydon, about 'a horrid morbidity of Temperament which has shown itself at intervals,'[65] he had already come to terms with melancholy as an integral part of his quest for the ideal of beauty. He affirms it in the same letter as he goes on to write, 'it is I have no doubt the greatest Enemy and stumbling block I have to fear.'[66] Composed much later, in May 1819, the *Ode on Melancholy* explores the relationship between joy and suffering in antithetical terms. This ambivalence or ambiguity of Melancholy is not only a source of mystery but as elusive and difficult to explain as some of Keats's other female figures like La Belle or Lamia.

In the first stanza of the ode, the poet rejects the stock conventional resources for arousing melancholy. He discards the path to Lethe and advocates a more arduous journey that would kindle 'the wakeful anguish of the soul' and intensify the experience of melancholy. Not only does Keats reject Lethe, nightshade, yew-berries but also the beetle, the death moth and the owl as they are likely to 'drown the wakeful anguish of the soul.'

However, the fit of melancholy falls all of a sudden. As Keats reveals in the second stanza,

But when the melancholy fit shall fall
    Sudden from heaven like a weeping cloud,
That fosters the droop-headed flowers all,
    And hides the green hill in an April shroud;

(*Ode on Melancholy*, Stz. II, 11-14)

The antithetical element of pursuit of melancholy becomes operative from this stanza onwards. We witness a series of contradictory ambiguities and antithetical assertions. As William Empson rightly points out in his discussion on the ode,

> ...Weeping produces the flowers of joy which are themselves sorrowful: the hill is green as young, fresh and springing, or with age, mould and geology: April is both rainy and part of spring time and the shroud, an anticipation of death that has its own energy and beauty, either is itself the fact that the old hill is hidden under green, or is itself the grey mist, the greyness of falling rain, which is reviving that Verdure...[67]

According to Empson, the poetic prescription of true melancholy and experience of life lies in this antithetical ambivalence of contraries. One is faced with two options. One either has to indulge in prolonged grief at the brevity of joy or beauty or fight out grief by indulging in the sheer intensity of experience.

Then glut thy sorrow on a morning rose,
    Or on the rainbow of the salt sand-wave,
    Or on the wealth of globed peonies;
Or if thy mistress some rich anger shows,
    Imprison her soft hand and let her rave,
    And feed deep, deep upon her peerless eyes.

(*Stanza*, II, 15-20)

Melancholy is all pervasive, from the beauty of the morning rose and rainbow to the 'wealth of globed peonies.' The aggressive lover would find it in the wrath laden eyes of his mistress. Feminine anger here is regarded as a rich spectacle for enjoyment. Such assertion implicitly affirms the futility of feminine anger, which is merely a cosmetic display-just a mere pretext to draw the attention of her lover. Endorsement of such feminine conduct is male chauvinistic and condescending with sadistic or sadomasochistic undertones. As regards the last three lines of the second stanza, Susan Wolfson points out something more important.

> ...We may think that the poem is prescribing an aesthetic ideology that denies woman's subjectivity with wilful restraint. But the real danger, it turns out, is the aesthete's self-cancelling devotion to a sensibility gendered as feminine : by the poem's close, it is 'She.' 'veiled Melancholy,' who is serene and self-contained and the male suitor who is appropriated and desubstantialised: "His soul shall taste the sadness of her might. And be among her cloudy trophies hung..."[68]

The association of melancholy with the 'rich anger' of the mistress gives way to the incarnation of the goddess in the third and final stanza. Unlike the *Ode to Psyche*, Keats in this ode does not direct any special effort to rescue the identity of the goddess for he sees and feels the presence of the goddess in all his pursuits of beauty, joy and pleasure. There is no need to separately pursue melancholy for it is inevitable in the quest of life. The pursuer does not shun beauty as a sort of protective mechanism against melancholy. On the contrary, he follows it with a greater zest: even if in such pursuit he is doomed forever. The recognition and discovery of 'Melancholy' in the final stanza is affirmed with the capitalization of the name.[69] She gets her recognition as 'a divine power austerely veiled.' The essence of beauty lies in its transience, as it is the quality of impermanence that accounts for the joy.

She dwells with Beauty-Beauty that must die;
And Joy, whose hand is ever at his lips
Bidding adieu; and aching Pleasure nigh,
Turning to poison while the bee-mouth sips.

(*Stanza* III, 21-24)

So in a true sense Keats ascribes only that beauty as authentic, which must perish, that joy as everlasting that must bid 'adieu,' and that pleasure as permanent which is 'aching.' 'This truth,' as Harold Bloom asserts,

> is seen by none except those who earn the poet's melancholy, which is not to be usurped. The strenuous tongue does not simply sip the grape's juice: it bursts the grape of Joy, with the inevitable double consequence of tasting might and the sadness of might. Moneta's or the Melancholy's double aspect, the Goddess as Muse and as a Destroyer. And be among her cloudy trophies hung....[70]

This ambivalent attitude of the pursuer which I have pointed out earlier is evident in the characterization of femininity in the Ode as well. As Empson points out,

> ...Opposite notions combined in this poem include death and the sexual act, a pair of which I must produce further examples: pain and pleasure, perhaps as a milder version of this: the conception of the woman as at once mistress and mother, at once soothing and exciting, whom one must master, to whom one must yield: a desire at once for the eternity of fame and for the irresponsibility of oblivion: and apprehension of ideal beauty and sensual: and an apprehension of eternal beauty as fleeting...[71]

The aspect of the female figure 'whom one must master, to whom one must yield' is crucially important for an understanding of Melancholy. We are reminded of the La Belle and Lamia. In the former this ambivalence is absolutely clear. At the beginning of the poem, as I have discussed already, it is the knight who is active in courtship. However, in the long run it is the female figure who gradually gains ascendancy and power. We find, a similar trend in the *Ode on Melancholy* as well. In the Ode the code of conduct prescribed at the end of the second stanza for the pursuer of melancholy, urges us to treat mistress's anger as a rich spectacle and snatch the initiative. It suggests an active role, but by the end of the final stanza the positions are totally reversed, with the female figure becoming triumphant, while the pursuer of the quest is merely reduced to one of her 'cloudy trophies.' As Dorothy Van Ghent points out,

> ...the image of sexual love—the central image of fertility, generation and vitality—tends to become a malignant disguise of death...[72]

The triumphant sway of the goddess is clearly revealed in the final two lines of the Ode.

> His soul shall taste the sadness of her might,
> And be among her cloudy trophies hung. (Stz. III, 29-30)

The word 'trophy' usually connotes triumph or success. But here it has a different twist associated with it. As Van Ghent points out,

> ...In Keats's ode, the trophy that the hero dedicates in the temple is also of an ideal character—his soul that is to say, a dedication of mind in its ideal capacity. The trophy figure corresponds with what Yeats called the "Mask," "that object of desire or moral ideal which is of all possible things the most difficult"—a "form created by passion to unite us to ourselves."[73]

When Keats says 'Beauty that must die,' at the beginning of the third stanza it has two implications. The first is the inevitability of death and the second the perception of beauty that blooms for a short span and then fades away stealing the strength and vitality of life. The second implication carries with it a sinister connotation that implies the destructive element of seduction and short lived ecstacy—a process in which the pursuer loses his self and ends up being a victim of the subject pursued.

So the *Ode on Melancholy* is quite complex as far as depiction of femininity goes. Here we witness the reversal process, where the male lover does not efface the female into a narcissistic self projection, but he himself gets consumed in the process. She is fatal, the poet is aware of it, yet he prescribes the experience of beauty without paying any heed whatsoever to the fact that he would definitely be 'among her cloudy trophies hung.' In this context Empson points out,

> ...Her trophies (death-pale are they all) and cloudy because vague and faint with the intensity and puzzling character of this fusion, or because already dead, or because, though preserved in verse, irrevocable. They are hung because sailors on escaping shipwreck hung up votive gifts in gratitude (Horace, III, i) or because, so far from having escaped, in the swoon of this achievement he has lost life, independence, and even distinction from her....[74]

We find a similar echo in Wolfson's words when she sees Melancholy as a figure of 'erotic entrapment and masculine self dissolution.'[75] Unlike in La Belle or Lamia, here we do not find any authoritative patriarchal voice condemning the female figure. So in a way, Keats in this ode approves of a female figure who has been given the prerogative to choose from experience and discard. There is an implicit sanction or affirmation of her independence, autonomy and free will. She is serene and self contained at the end of the poem. In *La Belle Dame Sans Merci* we witness the representatives of patriarchal society admonishing the knight at arms in dreams: in *Lamia*, Apollonius—the patriarchal authority, condemns Lycius against Lamia. In the *Ode on Melancholy* we have no such reprimands against the female figure. The masculine self undertakes the pursuit of Beauty at his own responsibility and ultimately dissolves in the female, losing his identity. Even if the male is doomed, the fault is entirely his and the female figure is not condemned for it by any patriarchal voice of authority. In an earlier version Keats intended to write, "His soul shall taste the anguish of her might." This anguish we can relate to the poet's prescription in the first stanza, 'wakeful anguish of the soul.' The word 'anguish' in all probability would have been more relevant keeping in view the nineteenth century position of women in contemporary society. The 'anguish' which is 'wakeful' lies in deliberate merging of the soul in the might of the Goddess by the pursuer of melancholy. In the process, masculinity with all its patriarchal biases has been dissolved in the feminine and we get a true taste of 'the sadness of her might.' In such dissolution we witness the emergence of a true emancipated liberated female who is serene, self controlled, powerful, independent and autonomous. Through such a depiction Keats indeed emerges as a pro-feminist—much ahead of his time.

NOTES

1. Karen Swann's essay, *Harassing The Muse in Rimanticism & Feminism* ed. Anne K. Mellor (Bloomington: Indiana University Press, 1988) p. 81.
2. Robert Graves, *The White Goddess: A Historical Grammar of Poetic Myth*, 2nd ed. (New York: Noonday Press, 1966) pp. 430-31.

   As cited in Dorothy Van Ghent's *Keats: The Myth of the Hero* (Princeton: New Jersey: Princeton UP, 1983) p. 128.
3. Van Ghent, *op. cit.*, p. 128.
4. Miriam Allott ed. *Keats: The Complete Poems* (1970: corr. Rpt. London: Longman, 1980) p. 503.
5. J.M. Murry. *Keats and Shakespeare* (London: OUP, 1925) p. 124.

   As cited in Leon Waldoff's *Keats and the Silent Work of Imagination* (Urbana & Chicago: University of Illinois Press, 1985) p. 83.
6. Robert Graves, *op. cit.*, pp. 430-31.

   As cited in Waldoff. *op. cit.*, p. 83.
7. Robert Gittings, *John Keats: The Living Year* (Cambridge, Mass: Harvard UP, 1954) pp. 120-123.

   As cited in Waldoff, *op. cit.*, p. 83.
8. Gittings. *John Keats*, p. 123.
9. Harold G. McCurdy's *La Belle Dame San's Merci* 171: cited in Waldoff. *op. cit.*, p. 83.
10. Susan J. Walfson's essay *Feminising Keats* in Peter J. Kitson ed. *New Caselooks: Coleridge, Keats and Shelley* (London: Macmillan Press Ltd. 1996) p. 103.
11. Gerald Enscoe, *Eros and the Romantics: Sexual Love as a theme in Coleridge, Shelley and Keats* (Hague, Netherlands: Mouton & Co. N.Y. Publishers, 1967) p. 141.
12. Wolfson, *op. cit.*, p. 103.
13. Anne K. Mellor, *Rimanticism & Gender* (London & New York: Routledge, 1993) p. 184.
14. Mellor, *Rimanticism & Gender*, p. 184.
15. Waldoff, *op. cit.*, pp. 85-86.
16. Waldoff, *op. cit.*, p. 87.

17. Holbrook Jackson ed. *The Anatomy of Melancholy* (New York: Vintage Books, 1977). III ("The Third Partition") p. 13.

    As cited in Waldoff. *op. cit.*, p. 87.

18. As cited in Waldoff. *op. cit.*, p. 88.

19. Robert Gittings ed., *Letters of John Keats* (1970: corr. rpt. Oxford: OUP, 1986) p. 136.

    Keats's letter to Benjamin Bailey 18, 22 July 1818.

20. Gittings. *Letters of John Keats,* p. 269.

    Keats's letter to Fanny Brawne 15(?) July 1819.

21. Waldoff. *op. cit.*, p. 91.

22. Mario L. D'Avanza, *Keats's Metaphors for the Poetic Imagination* (1967. rpt. Durham NC: Duke UP, 1971) p. 192.

23. D'Avanza. *Keats's Metaphors*, p. 200.

24. Newell Ford. *The Prefigurative Imagination of John Keats* (Hamden. Conn: Archon Books, 1966) p. 141.

    As cited in Judy Little's *Keats as a Narrative Poet. A Test of Invention* (Lincoln USA: University of Nebraska Press. 1975) p. 106.

25. Judy Little. *op. cit.*, p. 106.

26. Karen Swann, *op. cit.*, p. 84.

27. Karen Swann, *op. cit.*, p. 87.

28. Karen Swann, *op. cit.*, p. 90.

29. Karen Swann. *op. cit.*, p. 92.

30. Bhabatosh Chatterjee, *John Keats: His Mind and Work* (Bombay: Orient Longman, 1971) p. 125.

31. Enscoe, *op. cit.*, p. 150.

32. Bruce Clarke's essay, *Fabulous Monsters of Conscience: Anthropomophosis in Keats's Lamia in Studies in Romanticism* (Volume 23, No. 4. Winter 1984) published by The Graduate School. Boston University, p. 567.

33. Bruce Clarke, p. 574.

34. Bruce Clarke, p. 576.

35. Bruce Clarke, p. 576.

36. Enscoe, *op. cit.*, p. 152.

37. Earl Reeves Wasserman, *The Finer Tone: Keats's Major Poems* (1953: rpt. Baltimore: John Hopkins Press, 1960) p. 167.

38. Enscoe. *op. cit.*, p. 154.

39. Enscoe, pp. 154-155.

40. Enscoe, p. 155.

41. Enscoe, p. 158.
42. Waldoff, *op. cit.*, p. 167.
43. Waldoff, pp. 167-68.
44. Waldoff, p. 168.
45. Brian Stone, *The Potery of Keats* (London: Penguin Books, 1992) 96-97.
46. Waldoff, *op. cit.*, p. 168.
47. L. Trilling, *"The Fate of Pleasure" in Beyond Culture: Essays on Literature and Learning* (New York: Viking Press, 1955) p. 67.

    As cited in Waldoff. *op. cit.*, p. 168.
48. L. Trilling, p. 168.
49. L. Trilling, p. 170.
50. Clarence D. Thorpe, *The Mind of John Keats* (New York: OUP, 1926) p. 102.

    As cited in Enscoe. *op. cit.*, p. 143.
51. H.W. Garrod, Keats (Oxford: Clarendon Press. 1926) p. 62.

    As cited in Enscoe. *op. cit.*, p. 144.
52. R.D. Havens, "*Of Beauty and Reality in Keats*," ELH. XVII (1950). 209. As cited in Enscoe. *op. cit.*, p. 144.
53. Newell Ford, *The Prefigurative Imagination of Jolm Keats* (Stanford: Stanford UP, 1951) 144. As cited in Enscoe. *op. cit.*, p. 144.
54. Sidney Colvin. *John Keats: His Life and Poetry. His Friends Critics and After Fame* (London. 1917) pp. 407-408.

    As cited in Enscoe. *op. cit.*, pp. 144-45.
55. John University Murry, *Keats and Shakespeare* (London: OUP, 1926) p. 161.

    As cited in Waldoff. *op. cit.*, p. 170.
56. Douglas Bush, John Keats: His Life and Writings (New York: Macmillan 1966) p. 161.

    As cited in Waldoff. *op. cit.*, p. 170.
57. Freud. *On the Sexual Theories of Childfren* (Standard Edition. Ix. 216-17) and *On the Medusa's Head* (Standard Edition. XVIII. 273-74).

    As cited in Waldoff. *op. cit.*, p. 165.
58. Clarke. *op. cit.*, p. 563.
59. Clarke, p. 564.
60. Enscoe, *op. cit.*, p. 573.
61. Clarke, *op. cit.*, p. 573.

62. Enscoe, *op. cit.*, p. 164.
63. Clarke, *op. cit.*, pp. 576-77.
64. Robert Gittings. *John Keats* (1968: rpt. Middlesex: Penguin Books Ltd., 1985) p. 459.
65. Gittings ed. *Letters of John Keats*. p. 13.
    Keats's letter to B.R. Haydon 10, 11 May 1817.
66. Gittings., *Letters of John Keats*, p. 13.
67. William Empson. *Seven Types of Ambiguity* (1930: rpt. London: Penguin Books Ltd., 1995) p. 251.
68. Wolfson, *op. cit.*, p. 102.
69. Dorothy Van Ghent. *op. cit.*, p. 148.
70. Harold Bloom, *The Visionary Company: A Reading of English Romantic Poetry* (1961: rpt. Ithaca & London: Cornell UP, 1971) p. 416.
71. Empson, *op. cit.*, p. 250.
72. Van Ghent, *op. cit.*, p. 147.
73. Van Ghent, p. 154.
74. Empson, *op. cit.*, p. 252.
75. Wolfson, *op. cit.*, p. 102.

5

Gaining a Voice: Femininity in Endymion

BEGUN on 18 April 1817 at Carisbrooke, Isle of Wight and completed by 28 November 1817 at Burford Bridge, Surrey; Keats's *Endymion* belongs chronologically to an earlier phase of his poetic career. Yet in this poetic romance, the treatment of femininity is quite complex and interesting. It is probably the only work by Keats, which shows a gradual progression in the depiction of womanhood, from an idealistic and narcissistic self projection towards a more realistic, independent and autonomous version. In a way, the work depicts the growth and gradual maturity of the male personality—as the representative central male figure in the poetic narrative, is forced by circumstances to grow out of an idealist narcissistic vision of women to accept and embrace a more realistic and broad minded view of woman hood-as a 'valued other.'

In the first chapter of this thesis, I have already pointed out the biographical details of Keats's life and how they shaped his attitudes towards women. The relationship between mother and son, especially during infancy, childhood and the formative years, is crucially significant in psychoanalytic terms for the development and maturity of the male personality. Being doted upon in childhood, then abandoned and subsequently deserted for ever through death after a tragic return, Keats's mother deeply influenced and complicated the development of his poetic psyche. His diffidence, suspicious nature and vulnerability to anxiety in later life were all repurcussions of the deep rooted traumas he went through in his childhood. In the words of Barbara Schapiro, Keats's,

> Poetry expresses a struggle to relate to a mother who is not only literally dead, but who was effectively experienced as dead indifferent, untrust worthy, unloving-by the infant self... The infant's experience of the mother as its earliest love object deeply influences its experience of itself as a whole, coherent identity and its ability to perceive reality...[1]

Endymion's quest for the elusive Cynthia is an idealist quest which is dissociated from reality and sees womanhood as nothing but a narcissistic self projection. However, as I shall point out later on, by the end of the poem the narcissism gives away to a more mature, realistic vision of womanhood in the form of the Indian Maiden. Apart from Cynthia the poem abounds in women figures. Besides the Moon Goodess (called variously Diana, Cynthia, Phoebe and Moon) we have the anonymous golden haired maiden, Peona-Endymion's sister, Venus, Circe and the Indian maiden. I intend to discuss all these figures at length-on account of the significant roles they play in the poem-in this chapter of my thesis; but my primary focus will be on the two key female figures that account for the central ambiguity or enigma of the poem: Cynthia and the Indian maiden.

The Poetic romance starts off with Keats's famous exordium.

> A thing of beauty is a joy for ever:
> It's loveliness increases; it will never
> Pass into nothingness, but still will keep
> A bower just for us, and a sleep
> Full of sweet dreams, and health, and quiet breathing.
>
> (*Endymion,* I, 1-5)

The celebration of beauty at the start of the poem is not in terms of serene abstraction but in tune with concrete reality. Keats provides a list of shapes which all assert 'concrete and natural phenomena.'

> ... Such the sun, the moon,
> Trees, old and young, sprouting a shady boon
> For simple sheep; and such are daffodils
> With the green world they live in; and clear rills
> That for themselves a cooling covert make
> 'Gainst the hot season;
>
> (*Endymion,* I, 13-18)

How do we explain this concept of beauty? Beauty here involves internalization of an earlier experience and idealization of it. As Barbara Schapiro points out clearly, dismissing vague Neo platonic interpretation:

> Keats's conception of beauty as an internalized essence is not distract from, but is continuous with, his conception of its sensuous and erotic nature. By "beauty" Keats is basically referring to the experience of that first blissful harmony with our earliest love object and the subsequent internalization of that object as a "good" or idealized image. The specific associations in the first verse paragraph, the equation of beauty with a bower, with sleep and dreams, and, most significantly, with an "endless foundation" of drink "pouring" into us from above, all suggest the infant's experience at the breast. The second paragraph then describes how such an intense, erotically charged experience remains with us, becomes such a deep and integral part of us.[2]

This fact is clearly stated by Keats in the second stanza, as he declares:

> The passion poesy, glories infinite,
> Haunt us till they become a clearing light
> Unto our souls, and bound to us so fast
> That, whether there be shine or gloom o'ercast,
> They always must be with us, or we die.
>
> (Endymion, I, 29-33)

The last three lines reveal how these 'essences' of beauty are an integral part of the poet's psyche. They are internalized, so much so, that the very thought of their absence or disappearence conjures up images of death. So at the start of the poem, in concurrence with the thought of psychoanalytic critics, we can see that the pursuit of an ideal or true Beauty on the part of Endymion, is quintessentially nothing but an earnest attempt to reexperience or recover an idealised version of infantile love. This idealized version of love as manifested in the form of the goddess, is intimately bound with other allied elements like the mother image, narcissism and self centredness. As long as Endymion is obsessed with his impossible desire to recover that ideal infantile love, he is totally disillusioned and frustrated in his quest of the moon goddess. It is only much later when he is able to renounce the idealized vision that we witness 'a developing maturity and integration in the poet's self, in his ability to love and to accept separateness and reality.'[3]

On the mountain of Latmos, where the shepherds are euphoric in celebration of the feast of Pan we first encounter Endymion. He provides a sharp contrast to the ongoing celebration around. He is sensitive, alienated and solitary. The imagery testifies his suffering, though these are suggestions of his superiority over the rustic crowd.

His youth was fully blown,
Showing like Ganymede to manhood grown,
And, for those simple times, his garments were
A chieftain king's; beneath his breast, half bare,
Was hung a silver bugle, and between
His nervy knees there lay a boar-spear keen.
A smile was on his countenance; he seemed
To common lookers-on like one who dreamed
Of idleness in groves Elysian.
But there were some who feelingly could scan
A lurking trouble in his nether lip,
And see that oftentimes the reins would slip
Through his forgotten hands. Then would they sigh,
And think of yellow leaves, of owlets' cry,

> Of logs piled solemnly. Ah, well-a-day,
> Why should our young Endymion pine away?
>
> (*Endymion,* I, 169-84)

Endymion's gloominess is graphically stated in these lines. It clearly shows the sorry state which Endymion has sunk:

> ...the bugle and boar spear, symbols of the active, marital, and if the boar spear can be seen as a phallic image, the erotic life are hanging useless. He has no inclination to use either of them.[4]

A pall of gloom and melancholia hangs around Endymion, Keats relates his state with images of death and decay in nature,

> Then would they sigh,
> And think of yellow leaves, of owlets' cry,
> Of logs piled solemnly.
>
> (*Endymion*, I, 181-183)

Endymion's isolation is not only melancholic but it is narcissistic as well. In a way he is shut out of reality. The contrast is clearly depicted by Keats in these lines, as he says,

> Yet hourly had he striven
> To hide the cankering venom that had riven
> His fainting recollections. Now in deed
> His senses had swooned off; he did not heed
> The sudden silence, or the whispers low,
> Of the old eyes dissolving at his woe,
> Or anxious calls, or close of trembling palms,
> Or maiden's sigh, that grief itself embalms;
> But in the self-same fixed trance he kept,
> Like one who on the earth had never stepped.
> Aye, even as dead-still as a marble man,
> Frozen in that old tale Arabian.
>
> (*Endymion,* I, 395-406)

This narcissistic isolation is crucially important. If we trace the psychological strands, the roots of such narcissism lie in idealised infantile love. Through Endymion Keats explores the roots of such an 'unresolved infantile love relationship,'[5] and at the end shows that his ultimate redemption lies in acceptance of the Indian Maiden which in turn gives him freedom from 'his paralyzing narcissism.'[6]

Endymion ultimately reveals the source of his melancholy and depression to his sister Peona. But before that Peona whispers and gradually leads him to a 'cradling bower' or 'maternal nest' a congenial set up for his relaxation. It is here that Endymion falls asleep.

> O magic sleep! O comfortable bird,
> That broodest o'er the troubled sea of the mind
> Till it is hushed and smooth! O unconfined
> Restraint! Imprisoned Liberty! Great key
> To golden palaces, strange minstrelsy,
> Fountains grotesque, new trees, bespangled caves,
> Echoing grottoes, full of tumbling waves
> And moonlight-eye, to all the mazy world
> Of silvery enchantment!
>
> (*Endymion*, I, 453-461)

The sleep is not only magical but significant as well. According to psychoanalytic criticism,

> ...Sleep is a regression, a magic return to the idealized maternal environment. This sleep, he feels, "renovates" him, much as he feels the moon-goddess, who also comes upon him, in his sleep, is an "enchantment" that has "tortured" him with the promise of "renewed life" (918-19). Endymion's account of this torturous enchantment occupies the remainder of Book—I.[7]

The sheer presence of the moon goddess serves as a sort of enchantment. The maiden Endymion encounters in his dream, is beautiful in the erotic sense of the term.

> ....Yet she had,
> Indeed, locks bright enough to make me mad;
> And they were simply gordianed up and braided,
> Leaving, in naked comeliness, unshaded,

Her pearl-round ears, white neck, and orbed brow;
The which were blended in, I know not how,
With such a paradise of lips and eyes,
Blush-tinted cheeks, half smiles, and faintest sighs,
That, when I think thereon, my spirit clings
And plays about its fancy, till the stings
Of human neighbourhood envenom all.
....
....
..................Ah, see her hovering feet,
More bluely veined, more soft, more whitely sweet
Than those of sea-born Venus, when she rose
From out her cradle shell.

(*Endymion*, I, 612-27)

The ecstatic love making that follows is passionately sensuous. As in *Ode on Melancholy* or *Lamia,* the union is accompanied by the dissolution of the male in the female. The union seemed to him as a sort of surrender to death. Yet, she continues to be depicted in rather idealistic terms as she is referred to as 'that completed form of all completeness,' (BK—I line 606) and 'high perfection of all sweetness' (BK I line 607). The erotic union is vividly portrayed by Keats,

................Madly did I kiss
The wooing arms which held me, and did give
My eyes at once to death-but't was to live,
To take in draughts of life from the gold fount
Of kind and passionate looks, to count and count
The moments, by some greedy help that seemed
A second self, that each might be redeemed
And plundered of its load of blessedness,

(*Endymion,* I, 653-660)

In the light of psychoanalysis, the regressive element of the scene cannot be ignored.

> The regressive content in the scene is unmistakable. Especially revealing is the poet's feeling of a "second

> self" greedily plundering the erotic delights. One can understand that second self as the poet's subliminal infantile self hungrily engaging in greedy illicit feeling toward the mother. The fantasy, however, is dangerous and cannot be sustained : the goddess disappears and the dream falls "into nothing."[8]

To Peona, the dream is unhealthy and such vulnerability on the part of Endymion indicates the weakness of his character. She beckons him to discard the world of dreams and return to the pragmatic world of reality and manly action. Peona's concern for her brother is clearly revealed in the following lines, as she appeals to his masculinity, pride and sense of duty.

> At length, to break the pause,
> She said with trembling chance: 'Is this the cause?
> This all? Yet it is strange and sad, alas!
> That one who through this middle earth should pass
> Most like a sojourning demi-god, and leave
> His name upon the harp-string, should achieve
> No higher bard than simple maidenhood,
> Singing alone-and fearfully.
>
> (*Endymion,* I, 720-27)

Peona's revulsion at the obsessive dream that haunts Endymion is vividly brought out by Keats through stern words underlying her concern for such unhealthy behaviour. Her revulsion is clearly revealed in these lines.

> To put on such a look as would say, *Shame*
> *On this poor weakness*! (*Endymion,* I, 717-18)

Later she goes on to say,

> Then wherefore sully the entrusted gem
> Of high and noble life with thoughts so sick?
> Why pierce high-fronted honour to the quick.
> For nothing but a dream?
>
> (*Endymion,* I, 757-760)

Endymion defends himself in support of his dream vision. He tells Peona,

> Wherein lies happiness? In that which becks
> Our ready minds to fellowship divine,
> A fellowship with essence, till we shine
> Full alchemized, and free of space.
>
> (*Endymion,* I, 777-780)

The identification with this essence is evolved gradually. It owes its origin to the identification with natural objects like a rose leaf. The next step to such identification lies in journey through the world of music; at first the natural music, 'the free winds' ultimately gives way to human music in the form of songs. However, all these processes are gradually assimilated 'into a sort of oneness, and our state/Is like a floating spirit's.' (796-97). But this experience by degrees gives way to a 'Chief intensity.'

> To the Chief intensity the crown of these
> Is made of love and friendship. (*Endymion,* I, 800-801).

This divine essence in psychoanalytic terms is closely related to the ideal maternal image that he constantly pines for,

> 'That fellowship with essence and, more importantly, the divine "self destroying" love that he goes on to describe express a longing for a regressive fusion with the ideal mother.'[9]

In Keats's words

> All its more ponderous and bulky worth
> Is friendship, whence there ever issues forth
> A steady splendour; but at the tip-top
> There hangs by unseen film an orbed drop
> Of light, and that is love. Its influence,
> Thrown in our eyes, genders a novel sense,
> At which we start and fret, till in the end,
> Melting into its radiance, we blend,
> Mingle, and so become a part of it—

Nor with aught else can our souls interknit
So wingedly. When we combine therewith,
Life's self is nourished by its proper pith,
And we are nurtured like a pelican brood.
Aye, so delicious is the unsating food
That men, who might have towered in the Van
Of all the congregated world, to fan
And winnow from the coming step of time
All chaff of custom, wipe away all slime
Left by men-slugs and human serpentry,
Have been content to let occaion die,
Whilst they did sleep in love's elysium.

(*Endymion,* I, 803-823)

The imagery here strongly underlines the regressive fusing nature of love. The search for the ideal mother is revealed in the images, ' "orbed drop" of love which certainly suggests breast/ milk, and the self is explicitly "nourished" and "nurtured" by this love.'[10] The love is not only regressive but narcissistic as well, and it is clearly revealed at the end of Book—I, when Endymion tells Peona that on coming upon the water in the well, he saw the same beautiful face he had seen in his dreams, in his reflection in the water.

And, therefore, just going, when, behold,
A wonder, fair as any I have told—
The same bright face I tasted in my sleep,
Smiling in the clear well.

(*Endymion,* I, 893-96)

The goddess's face here is seen by the poet in his own reflection. So the love for the goddess is in reality a love for an ideal self. We are reminded of the similar narcissistic vision in the well in Shelley's *Alastor* (lines 479-92).

A spirit seemed
To stand beside him clothed in no bright robes
Of shadowy silver or enshrining light.

....
....
To beckon him.

So does Keats advocate a regressive narcissistic fusing love through Endymion? No, on the contrary, Keats through the poem asserts the need to give up such a futile, selfcentred, idealistic vision and engage in a more fulfilling, socially oriented, mature reality which gives recognition and autonomy to women as a valued other.

In the second book, Endymion journeys down into the deeper regions of earth in search of his love. He prays to Cynthia to reduce her torment and to grant him power to fly and fulfil his desire for union with the goddess. The region he roams about is

...Dark, nor light,
The region; nor bright, nor sombre wholly,
But mingled up; a gleaming melancholy;
A dusky empire and its diadems;
One faint eternal eventide of gems.

(*Endymion,* II, 221-225)

The images of the under world that we get are death like, cold, melancholic and sombre. Phrases like 'chilly and numb' (II. line-243) 'fathomless and dim'(II. line 272); ' wild uncertainty and shadows grim' (II. line 273) underline the gloominess of the underworld. He realizes the futility of his aimless roamings deep inside the cold, lifeless and gloomy labyrinthine underground corridors. As the poet says,

The journey homeward to habitual self!
A mad pursuing of the fog-born elf,
Whose flitting lantern, through rude nettle-briar,
Cheats us into a swamp, into a fire,
Into the bosom of a hated thing. (*Endymion,* II, 276-80)

In psychoanalytic terms we can interpret this journey as a recoil into his ownself. As a Barbara Schapiro points out,

...The poet's journey into the maternal earth is also a journey into the self. The "dusky empire" reflects the

> murky, dissociated landscape of the poet's internal world of object relations. Thus, the cold and unresponsive, deathlike realm he has traversed only leads him back along a "crude and sore" path to a "hated" self...[11]

With Endymion's prayer to Diana we witness a gradual change in the atmosphere. The cold dead milieu gives way to "leaves...flowers, and wreaths, and ready myrtle crowns" (11.341-42). It is amidst these circumstances that he comes across the bower of Venus and Adonis. The sensuous pleasures of this place are described in detail by Keats, as Endymion sees the enactment of the Venus-Adonis myth after the annual reawakening of Adonis. The mythic enactment is followed by the blessing of Venus which assures Endymion of optimism and ultimate success in the quest of life. After this we witness the short appearance of Cynthia that culminates in passionate love making with Endymion.

> Long time ere silence did their anxious fears
> Question that thus it was; long time they lay
> Fondling and kissing every doubt away;
> Long time ere soft caressing sobs began
> To mellow into words, and then there ran
> Two bubbling springs of talk from their sweet lips.
>
> (*Endymion,* II, 733-38)

Cynthia assures Endymion that he would be blessed and immortalized through steadfast devotion to his quest of love. The magic of kiss would transform him,

> ....Now a soft kiss...
> Aye, by that kiss I vow an endless bliss,
> An immortality of passions's thine.
> Ere long I will exalt thee to the shine
> Of heaven ambrosial, and we will shade
> Ourselves whole summers by a river glade,
> And I will tell thee stories of the sky,
> And breathe thee whispers of its minstrelsy.
>
> (*Endymion,* II, 806-813)

Once again we witness, evidences of the dissolution of the male in the female, as in his idealized quest Endymion yearns to dissolve in the moon goddess. As he says, he wants 'to melt', to 'entwine hoveringly.'

> My happy love will overwing all bounds!
> Oh, let me melt into thee, let the sounds
> Of our close voices marry at their birth.
> Let us entwine hoveringly—
>
> (*Endymion,* II, 814-17)

The second book ends with Endymion's hearing the lament of ever parted lovers, the river god Alpheus and the stream nymph Aresthusa. Endymion earnestly prays to his goddess to unite the parted lovers and for the first time, we witness Endymion coming out of his narcissism with genuine concern for others. As Endymion prays,

> ....On the verge
> Of that dark gulf he wept, and said, 'I urge
> Thee, gentle Goddess of my pilgrimage,
> By our eternal hopes, to soothe, to assuage,
> In thou art powerful, these lovers' pains,
> And make them happy in some happy plains.'
>
> (*Endymion,* II, 1012-1017)

So what transformation do we see in Endymion at the end of second Book. At the end of second book, though Endymion

> is still obsessed with his goddess at the completion of this stage of his journey, his ability at the end to focus on an unhappy love besides his own, to recognize that he is not alone in his suffering, and indeed to pray to his goddess not for his own but for the happiness of others, suggests some progress in the poet's inner journey of self integration and maturation.[12]

So in a way it is the first step to move out of narcisstic isolation, empathize with others sufferings and genuinely wish and pray for the union of Alpheus and Aresthusa.

In the third book, Endymion matures even more as he encounters a father figure in the old man Glaucus that further aids him in detaching himself from the idealistic maternal fixation and obsessive narcissism. There is a great deal of similarity between Glaucus and Endymion. The old man of the sea is under the spell of a seductress called Circe. Endymion quite naturally empathizes with him, for as a youngman, Glaucus too felt the yearning for the sea like Endymion.

> .... I began
> To feel distempered longings, to desire
> The utmost privilege that ocean's sire
> Could grant in benediction—to be free
> Of all his kingdom.
>
> (*Endymion,* III, 375-78)

Glaucus realizes the futility of narrating the details of the deeper maternal regions, as Endymion himself has journeyed through them.

> .... And at once I visited
> The ceaseless wonders of this ocean-bed,
> No need to tell thee of them, for I see
> That thou hast been a witness—it must be;
>
> (*Endymion,* III, 391-394)

Like Endymion's love for Cynthia, Glaucus too pursued his elusive love for Scylla in the deeper regions of the earth. The search for Scylla, landed Glaucus in the bower of Circe-the 'cruel enchantress.'Circe comes to Glaucus disguised in the form of an ideal mother. Maternal images are recurrent as Glaucus says,

> Who could resist? Who in this universe?
> She did so breathe ambrosia, so immerse
> My fine existence in a golden clime.
> She took me like a child of suckling time,
> And cradled me in roses.
>
> (*Endymion,* III, 453-57)

After pouring maternal affection, she disappears only to return with venom.

> .....Fierce, wan
> And tyrannizing was the lady's look,
> As over them a gnarled staff she shook,
>
> (*Endymion,* III, 506-508)

The consequences of her tyranny were fatal for Glaucus. Amidst 'vast and desolate and icycold' (III. 632) surroundings he felt his limbs become 'Gaunt, withered, sapless, feeble, cramped, and lame.' (III. 638). It is Glaucus's belief that he has to pay a heavy price for initially giving into the 'idyllic maternal love'[13] promised by Circe. As I have pointed out earlier, Glaucus finds the call of maternal love irresistible, yet there is something wrong in it.

> Glaucus thus senses that in his love for the goddess there is something illicit, punishable. He is indeed punished for the destructive rage that lurks in his love for the mother. Endymion, he believes, is the "restoring chance."[14]

Circe's earlier victims have been hypnotized by her. She resorts to narcotics and poison to transform the whole clan of her victims into a phantom snake. When it comes to her knowledge that Glaucus has seen all this, she immediately takes revenge by turning him into a dying old man, 'gaunt, wither'd, sapless, feeble, cramp'd and lame.' So yielding to the initial maternal charms only retards the realization of quest of love. It ends in frustration as it only ends in 'powerlessness and withered age,' and 'represents a caricature of the whole notion of the romantic quest.'[15] So through the Circe-Glaucus episode, Keats once again depicts the futility of pursuit of narcissistic regressive fusing love with craving for infantile maternal pleasures; that often mount to idealism dissociated from reality and autonomous vision of women.

The alliance of Glaucus with Endymion, as regards love for the mother image is further enhanced when we hear Endymion uttering in joy, 'We are twin brothers in this destiny!' (III. 713).

Endymion being the redeemer is led by Glaucus to the caverns, where the dead lovers are to be resurrected at his intervention. In accordance with Glaucus's instructions Endymion redeems the dead lovers by scattering the torn pieces of the old man's scroll on them, following which they awaken and euphorically celebrate their triumph over death. The jubilant reunited lovers rush into celebrate victory at Neptune's palace, where Endymion falls asleep and is reassured by Venus of success in his dream. The imagery is once again strongly maternal.

'Oh, I shall die! Sweet Venus, be my stay!
Where is my lovely mistress? Well-away!
I die-I hear her voice-I fell my wing—'
At Neptune's feet he sank. A sudden ring
Of Nereids were about him in kind strife
To Usher back his spirit into life.
But still he slept. At last they interwove
Their cradling arms, and purposed to convey
Towards a crystal bower far away.

(*Endymion,* III, 1010-1018)

The strong maternal images ['cradling arms,' a crystal bower] underline the fact that 'Endymion is obviously still self destructively attached to the image of the ideal mother.'[16] Yet he progresses and matures a lot, his involvement in redeeming other characters shows his gradual overcoming of narcissism and active realistic dealing with other sufferers.

Book IV finds Endymion back on earth where he hears the griefstricken lament mourning the loss of home and friends. Overhearing the alienated cry, Endymion empathizes with it and experiences a "kindred pain." Investigating the source, Endymion comes across the Indian Maiden and spontaneously falls in love with her being over whelmed by her beauty. Yet he feels torn apart 'between loyalty and love for Cynthia and this spontaneous, uncontrollable desire for the beautiful maiden.'[17]

Upon a bough
He leant, wretched. He surely cannot now

Thirst for another love. Oh, impious,
That he can even dream upon it thus!
Thought he, 'Why am I not as are the dead,
Since to a woe like this I have been led
Through the dark earth and through the wondrous sea?
Goddess, I love thee not the less!...
....
....
For both, for both my love is so immense,
I feel my heart is cut for them in twain.'

(*Endymion,* IV, 86-97)

The painful conflict torments Endymion. He is torn apart between his attraction for Cynthia and the Indian Maiden. He ultimately comes to terms with reality and decides to live with the Indian maiden on earth. Yet, the Indian maiden refuses to give in 'insisting that she is forbidden to yield to him.'[18] Following this, Endymion decides to give up everything and lead the life of a hermit. It is at this juncture that Cynthia appears and resolves the crisis by stating that both she and the Indian maiden are the same. Both these female figures merge, and Endymion fades away with the Indian maid to dwell in the forests of Latmos and live happily everafter.

We are confronted with a lot of confusions at the end of the poem. Who is this Indian maiden? Is she an earthly manifestation of the ideal or some other entity? The confusions are best resolved only by psychoanalytic and not Platonist explanations. The suffering of Endymion that we encounter earlier is nothing but a 'painful acceptance of aloneness and the impossibility of recovering an infantile fusion with the mother.'[19]At the start of Book four, Endymion's return to mother earth reveals the growth of his maturity and his empathy with the Indian maiden shows how he crawls out of his narcissistic alienation and leaves behind his idealistic maternal obsessions to indulge in real human relationships. Endymion's feelings of guilt and confusion are an integral part of his growth of personality. That Endymion genuinely intends to discard the self destructive narcissistic love and embrace a more constrained but genuine cherishing of real love of another independent autonomous female, is revealed in his horror at his own realization of the narcissistic nature of his love. He realizes this with the disappearance of the Indian maiden.

> Despair! Despair!
> He saw her body fading gaunt and spare
> In the cold moonshine, Straight he seized her wrist;
> It melted from his grasp. Her hand he kissed,
> And, horror, kissed his own—he was alone.
>
> (*Endymion,* IV, 506-10)

Endymion's apprehensions and horrors give way with the return of the Indian Maid. He now genuinely feels her necessity, He gets a new lease of life, as he says,

> Now I see
> The grass, I feel the solid ground, Ah, me!
> It is thy voice-divinest! Where? Who, who
> Left thee so quiet on this bed of dew?
> Behold upon this happy earth we are.
> Let us ay love each other. Let us fare
> On forest-fruits, and never, never go
> Among the abodes of mortals here below,
> Or be by phantoms duped.
>
> (*Endymion*, IV, 621-29)

Having accepted a realistic version of love and attained fulfilment. Endymion now explains the futility of having self destructively trapped himself in an idealised narcissistic love. The futility of clinging to the ideal mother image is revealed as he goes on to say,

> I have clung
> To nothing, loved a nothing, nothing seen
> Or felt but a great dream! Oh, I have seen
> Presumptuous against love, against the sky,

Against all elements, against the tie
Of mortals each to each,...

(*Endymion,* IV, 636—641)

The unnatural nature and impossibility of such self destructive love is also admitted by Endymion,

.... So my story
Will I to children utter, and repent.
There never lived a mortal man who bent
His appetite beyond his natural sphere
But starved and died.

(*Endymion,* IV, 644-48)

Such unnatural love will only bring repentance, starvation and death. He looks upon Indian maiden as the redeemer, a saviour who can save him from such self destructive narcissistic love and teach him to accept femininity-not as an idealised self projection but an autonomous reality.

My Sweetest Indian, here,
Here will I kneel, for thou redeemed hast
My life from too thin breathing, Gone and past
Are cloudy phantasms.

(*Endymion*, IV, 648-651)

He discards his dreams and fantasies and accepts reality.

My Indian bliss!
My river-lily bud!One human kiss!
One sigh of real breath-one gentle squeeze,
Warm as a dove's nest among summer trees,
And Warm with dew at ooze from living blood!
Whither didst melt? Ah, what of that! All good
We'll talk about—no more of dreaming....

(*Endymion,* IV, 663-69)

Though he is willing to abandon his dreams and fantasies and dwell in a realistic world of love, Endymion is still refused by the Indian maiden as she insists that she has been forbidden by some enigmatic decree to yield to him. Before the final triumph of love, Endymion once again has to encounter alienation and bewilderment. He firmly decides to discard the Maiden and live a hermetic life, as he tells his sister Peona.

> Let it content thee, sister, seeing me
> More happy than betides mortality.
> A hermit young, I'll live in mossy cave,
> Where thou alone shalt come to me and lave
> Thy spirit in the wonders I shall tell.
>
> (*Endymion,* IV, 858-862)

The dilemma is ultimately resolved as the idealised vision of Cynthia unites with the Indian Maiden, and Endymion abandons his hermetic existence to be united with her. According to Aileen Ward, Endymion,

> finally realizes that to renounce the maid is to deny life itself, he is rewarded by the maid's transformation into the goddess, that is, real love, when accepted for the good it contains, leads to the fulfilment Endymion has sought all along.[20]

So we see in Endymion, Keats prescribed acceptance of womanhood as an independent, autonomous and free entity. After a lot of struggle Endymion ultimately succeeds in giving 'the woman wholeness and reality.' The narcissist male protagonist at the start of the poem who is preoccupied with his idealizations and fantasies of the mother and self is made to overcome and resist 'a pull toward a regressive fusing love' and give autonomy to women at the end. When Anne K. Mellor charges Romantic male poets as narcissistic self lovers, she is not wrong, as she asserts,

> The most famous Romantic love poems may thus propound a sexism of a most seductive and insidious kind for the poet claims to cherish his beloved, bright star that she is above all else. But the love he feels is but self love; he ignores her human otherness in order impose his own metaphors, his own identity, upon her, to render her but a clone (or soul mate) of himself. What he most deeply

> desires is absolute possession of the beloved; but since this desire is never realizable in life, his quest always fails leaving him frustrated, forlorn, sinking, trembling, expiring, yet still yearning for his impossible ideal.[21]

But Keats through Endymion ultimately forces the male protagonist to give up the self destructive narcissistic love and accept the female as the valued other-free, independent and different. Cynthia and the Indian maid represent two opposite strands of the Romantic vision of Keats. The former is an idealistic creation of narcissism built on the infantile yearning for regressive fusing love for mother; while the latter is a creation based on acceptance of a more realistic emancipated version of woman hood—which breaks the shackles of self centredness and gives a new kind of relatedness to society, based on independence of the female. It envisages a society where women have equal rights as their male counterpart, and in that context Keats emerges as a profeminist.

NOTES

1. Barbara A. Schapiro, *The Romantic Mother: Narcissistic Patterns in Romantic Poetry* (Baltimore: John Hopkins UP, 1983) p. 38.
2. Barbara A. Schapiro, *The Romantic Mother: Narcissistic Patterns in Romantic Poetry* (Baltimore: John Hopkins UP, 1983) pp. 40-41.
3. Barbara A. Schapiro, *The Romantic Mother: Narcissistic Patterns in Romantic Poetry* (Baltimore: John Hopkins UP, 1983) p. 41.
4. Gerald Enscoe, *Eros and the Ramantics, Sexual Love as a theme in Coleridge. Shelley and Keats* (Hague, Netherlands: Mouton & Co. N.V. Publishers 1967) p. 108.
5. Schapiro, *op. cit.,* p. 42.
6. Schapiro, *op. cit.,* p. 42.
7. Schapiro, *op. cit.,* p. 42.
8. Schapiro, *op. cit.,* p. 43.
9. Schapiro, *op. cit.,* p. 44.
10. Schapiro, *op. cit.,* p. 45.
11. Schapiro, *op. cit.,* pp. 46-47.
12. Schapiro, *op. cit.,* p. 48.
13. Schapiro, *op. cit.,* p. 49.

14. Schapiro, *op. cit.,* p. 49.
15. Stuart M. Sperry Jnr's essay, *The Allegory of Endymion* in John Spencer Hill ed., *Keats: The Narrative Poems, A Casebook* (London and Basingstoke: The Macmillan Press Ltd., 1983) p. 96.
16. Schapiro, *op. cit.,* p. 49.
17. Enscoe, *op. cit.,* p. 121.
18. Enscoe, *op. cit.,* p. 122.
19. Schapiro, *op. cit.,* p. 50.
20. Aileen Ward, *John Keats : The Making of a Poet* (1963: rpt. Canada: Collins Publishers Toronto, 1986) p. 143.
21. Anne K. Mellor, *Romanticism & Gender* (London & New York: Routledge, 1993) p. 27.

6

Voice of Autonomy: Moneta

FEMALE figures abound in Keats's attempts at composing full fledged epics in the form of *Hyperion* and *The Fall of Hyperion*. We meet the daughters of Earth and Heaven and other allied female figures — Thea, Cybele, Themis, Phoebe, Thethys, Clymene, Asia and Ops. However, in this chapter I intend to discuss two of the major classical female figures, rather the two forms in which they appear: Mnemosyne and Moneta. Other female figures fade into insignificance as Mnemosyne (in *Hyperion*) and later Moneta (in *The Fall of Hyperion*) reigns supreme in the epics; being the dominant, autonomous, female forces drawing our critical attention. Both teach words of wisdom, knowledge and humanity to male poet.

We first meet Mnemosyne in the narrative when she approaches grieving Apollo and asks him the reasons for his grief,

> Show thy heart's secret to an ancient Power
> Who hath forsaken old and sacred thrones
> For prophecies of thee, and for the sake
> Of loveliness newborn.

[*Hyperion*, III, 76-79]

It is Apollo's 'aching ignorance' that made him miserable and melancholic and it is only on reading a 'wondrous lesson' in Mnemosyne's face that he gains immortality. Apollo's encounter with Mnemosyne and his transfiguration are in all probability, allegorical representations of Keats's own emergence as a true poet—a poet who would now deal with the reality of human suffering, rather than seek escape in a world of dreams. Mnemosyne presides over this transformation of Apollo. She is herself a Titan, yet as goddess of memory and mother of the Muses she plays a crucial role. She predicts the rise of a new god, whose creative purpose is asserted by the possession of a lyre.

Before appearing in reality, Mnemosyne prophesied her arrival to Apollo through dreams. When Apollo awoke from his dream, he found beside him a magical lyre-on playing upon which Apollo mesmerized the entire universe. The path to wisdom is inextricably bound with that of suffering. Apollo's restlessness and central queries about truth of life cannot be answered but only perceived in the deepest core of life and existence. The realization and perception of wisdom for Apollo is almost like going through the process of death and being reborn.

> Soon wild commotions shook him, and made flush
> All the immortal fairness of his limbs—
> Most like the struggle at the gate of death;
> Or liker still to one who should take leave
> Of pale immortal death, and with a pang
> As hot as death's is chill, with fierce convulse
> Die into life. So young Apollo anguished;
> His very hair, his golden tresses famed,
> Kept undulation round his eager neck.
> During the pain Mnemosyne upheld
> Her arms as one who prophesied.
>
> [*Hyperion*, III, 124-134]

Mnemosyne is representative of the new religion of beauty. She is the incarnation of wisdom and the essence of life to Apollo. She is also like a mother figure comforting her child in distress. She is not an 'admonitory figure' like Moneta in *The Fall of Hyperion*. According to Harold Bloom,

> ...She figures as a preceptress without needing to say anything; her lesson is in her face, as the final truth taught by Moneta will become clear in an unveiling of her countenance.[1]

Mnemosyne's maternal role takes on a new dimension altogether in Moneta, whom we meet in *The Fall of Hyperion*. The obsessive infantile dilemmas concerning mother, which we have seen in *Endymion* return here. The narrative opens in an idealized maternal set up and the poet falls asleep after consuming a 'cool vessel of transparent juice.' Though there is a change in milieu after the poet awakens—from abundant vegetative imagery to a marble environment—yet, maternal images continue to dominate.

The onward journey is similar to the one Endymion undertakes, down into the nether region of the earth. Being transported to a colossal temple his gaze falls on a large, 'image huge of feature as a cloud,' at whose altar a priestess is burning incense. It is here that he hears a voice proclaiming his demise, if he did not immediately follow the steps to the altar. Endeavouring to do so, the poet felt 'a palsied chill' that struck through his limbs as he struggled against the numbness of death. In the light of psychoanalytic criticism:

> ...The poet's ability simply to face and experience these cold and hateful feelings, however, is itself a first step toward self-integration and maturity.[2]

This experience can also be compared to that of Apollo at the end of *Hyperion*, before Mnemosyne prophesies to him,

> Slow, heavy, deadly was my page; the cold
> Grew stifling, suffocating, at the heart;
> And when I clasped my hand I felt them not,
> One minute before death, my iced foot touched
> The lowest stair; and as it touched, life seemed
> To pour in at the toes.

[*The Fall of Hyperion*, I, 129-134]

As Apollo asked Mnemosyne to be relieved of misery in *Hyperion*, the pilgrim here too asks,

….. 'High Prophetess,' said I, 'purge off,
Benign, if so it please thee, my mind's film.'

[*The Fall of Hyperion*, I, 145-46]

The remedy lies in empathizing with misery of humanity,

'None can usurp this height,' returned that shade,
'But those to whom the miseries of the world
Are misery, and will not let them rest.
All else who find a haven in the world,
Where they may thoughtless sleep away their days,
If by a chance into this fame they come,
Rot on the pavement where thou rotted' st half,'

[*The Fall of Hyperion*, I, 146-153]

When Moneta admonishes him in lines 161-69, we find her accusing the poet of 'narcissistic idealism,' being alienated from the mainstream of humanity. This is precisely what Moneta implies when she rebukes the poet by referring to him as 'a dreaming thing,' 'a fever of thyself' in the following lines,

'Those whom thou spak'st of are no visionaries,'
Rejoined that voice, They are no dreamers weak,
They seek no wonder but the human face;
No music but a happy—noted voice—
They come not here, they have no thought to come—
And thou art here, for thou art less than they,
What benefit canst thou do, or all thy tribe,
To the great world? Thou art a dreaming thing,
A fever of thyself. Think of the earth;
What bliss even in hope is there for thee?
What haven?….

[*The Fall of Hyperion*, I, 161-171]

This element of narcissism has been rightly pointed out by Barbara A Schapiro,

…The poet is accused of the same unhealthy, culpable behaviour as Endymion: he is condemned for his narcissistic idealism. By chasing after his own fantasies and idealizations. He is betraying both the real world-the

> Earth, his true "home"—and humankind. Keats reveals an awareness of the self destructive, masochistic nature of this narcissistic idealism.[3]

In *The Fall of Hyperion* Keats distinguishes between the poet and the dreamer. The poet does not remain trapped within his own self but is 'a sage, A humanist physician to all men.' [*The Fall of Hyperion*, 1, 189-90]. The poet is opposed to the dreamer: 'The one pours out a balm upon the world. The other vexes it?' [*The Fall of Hyperion*, I, 201-202].

With these central realizations and reflections of life, Keats is finally prepared to face the 'Majestic shadow,' as he asks her to unfold her mystery to him.

> 'Majestic shadow, tell me where I am,
> Whose alter this; for whom this incense curls;
> What image this whose face I cannot see,
> For the broad marble knees, and who thou art,
> Of accent feminine, so courteous?'
>
> [*The Fall of Hyperion*, I, 211-15]

Moneta reveals her identity as the 'Sole priestess of his desolation' (line 227). The description of Moneta's face is one of the most powerful passages in Keatsian verse.

> .....Then saw I a wan face,
> Not pined by human sorrows, but bright-blanched
> By an immortal sickness which kills not.
> It works a constant change, which happy death
> Can put no end to; deathwards progressing
> To no death was that visage, it had passed
> The lily and the snow; and beyond these
> I must not think now, though I saw that face—
> But for her eyes I should have fled away.
> They held me back, with a benignant light,
> Soft mitigated by divinest lids
> Half-closed, and visionless entire they seemed
> Of all external things-they saw me not,
> But in blank splendour beamed like the mild moon,

Who comforts those she sees not, who knows not
What eyes are upward cast....

[*The Fall of Hyperion,* I, 256-271]

We witness contraries in the description, as death and loss are associated with love and pity. It is the poet's ultimate acceptance of reality of life that embraces both creation and decay, joy and pain, and finally sustenance and despondency. Such an acceptance of reality, helps the poet to move out of his self destructive narcissism and gain a new relatedness to the world. It embraces the realism of human suffering and misery. The poet gradually journeys from suffering to knowledge.

I ached to see what things the hollow brain
Behind enwombed; what high tragedy
In the dark secret chambers of her skull.

[*The Fall of Hyperion*, I, 276-78]

Moneta shows a path of knowledge that journeys through pain and suffering. It assures immortality in a impersonal, yet generous manner, through the cult of humanism. The male poet is empowered to transform 'with an electral changing misery' (line 246). Moneta's curse to a work of wonder and,

'My power, which to me is still a curse,
Shall be to thee a wonder; for the scenes
Still swooning vivid through my globed brain,
With an electral changing misery,
Thou shalt with these dull mortal eyes behold,
Free from all pain, if wonder pain thee not.'

[*The Fall of Hyperion*, I, 243-248]

So the characterization of Moneta reveals a certain amount of ambivalence in Keatsian attitude towards femininity. In his grand heroic attempt at writing Miltonic epic-which, as I have already pointed out earlier, is a form of masculine assertion as compared to the feminine forms of odes, ballads and sonnets; he endows all wisdom and knowledge to his central female figure Moneta. Yet, it is the task of the male poet to transform 'that feminine historic and graphic consciousness into an adequate poetic language?' As Anne K Mellor further points out,

> ...Here the visual (the face of Moneta) and the verbal (the discourse of the male poet) finally fuse, in Keats's emblematic description of Moneta's "bright—blanch'd" face "death wards progressing/To no death." The male poet thus achieves an enduring relationship of equality and difference with the female divinity. Having approached the goddess like a child to his mother, reaching only to her "board marble knees" (I:214) and hearing her "immortals's sphered words" softened "to an mother's" (I:250), having gazed upon her sublime face, the poet narrator "ached to see what things the hollow brain/Behind enwombed" (I:287) .....Through "daring" and the courage to suffer "without stay or prop....The load of this eternal quietude" (I:388-90), the male poet discovers what is ultimately for Keats the appropriate relationship between female and male in poetic discourse: that of goddess/mother/muse to human/son/poet, a relationship that sustains the role of humble submission and dependency Keats has everywhere adopted in relation to feminine creative power....[4]

So, in Moneta, irrespective of the complexities, we find the best example of a powerful, immortal, autonomous and independent woman who can teach the male poet words of wisdom. She is the messenger of humanity. She accounts for the transcendence of the male poet. It is due to her admonishment and words of wisdom that the poet is able to break the shackles of egocentricity and accept a more realistic viewpoint of the world based on humanism. She embodies both the tenderness and affection of a mother, as well as, the sternness and impersonal detachment of an autonomous, independent woman who preaches altruism. Her embodiment is based on contraries, contraries that ultimately lead to progression, self knowledge and socialization of the male poet.

NOTES

1. Harold Bloom, *The Visionary Company: A Reading of English Romantic Poetry* (1961: rpt. New York: Cornell UP, 1971) p. 397.
2. Barbara A. Schapiro, *The Romantic Mother: Narcissistic Patterns in Romantic Poetry*, (Baltimore: John Hopkins UP, 1983) p. 56.
3. Barbara A. Schapiro, *The Romantic Mother: Narcissistic Patterns in Romantic Poetry*, (Baltimore: John Hopkins UP, 1983) p. 57.
4. Anne K. Mellor, *Romanticism and Gender* (London & New York: Routledge, 1993) p. 185.

Conclusion

IN my earlier chapters I have discussed various women figures in Keats's verse. In my final chapter, I shall try to assemble the inferences that we can draw from these depictions. What conclusions can we really arrive at from Keats's depiction of these women figures in verse?

Once again Keats defies any definite form of classification, especially as regards his attitude towards the opposite sex. We can neither brand him exclusively as a feminist nor can we slot him with other male Romantic poets—who have been accused of being oblivious of the presence of the female, as an autonomous entity in poetic discourse by feminist critics.[1] A study of Keats's women figures re-inforces the observations made in the second chapter of the book, that his is a special case especially as regards studies in gender and feminism are concerned. In Keats we find a blending of both conventional male attitudes along with observations that see women as the 'valued other.' It is for this reason that Anne K Mellor, in her work *Romanticism & Gender*, refers to Keats as an 'ideological crossdresser.'[2] who takes on traits of feminine Romanticism. Yet such crossdressing in an outcome of a complex network of social and personal circumstances, to which I have drawn attention. Keats's marginalized existence like women due to low social origin, his poetic prescription of 'negative capability' which implies empathy or 'weak ego boundaries' and indirectly aligns him with the female; the hostile charges of effeminacy by contemporary reviewers and contemporaries like Hunt, Byron and Hazlitt; and finally Shelley's funeral elegy '*Adonais*' that exacerbated the charge of effeminacy on Keats—are just some of the circumstances that contributed to his own complex attitude towards gender and women.

So in Keats, while on the one hand we have autonomous, independent female figures like Melancholy, Moneta and the Indian Maiden; on the other hand, Keats disapproved of some independent, wilful female characters like La Belle and Lamia. As feminist critics[3] argue, whenever women appear in Romantic verse as autonomous, independent and assertive they are either demonized with ambiguity like (Geraldine in Coleridge's *Christabel*) or eradicated and overcome. Inspite of creating independent women figures like Moneta and Melancholy, Keats puzzles us by aligning himself with the conventional attitude of the Romantic male—that sees the liberated, independent woman as a threat to the patriarchal society and has to be overcome by any means. We find such instances in La Belle and Lamia. In the latter by making the central female character ambiguous he aligns Lamia with a character like Geraldine, whom we meet in Coleridge's *Christabel*. Being helplessly cornered into the position of the androgynous passive poet, Keats even internalized some of his figures. This I have already pointed out in *Ode to Psyche* where he identifies with and internalizes Psyche. Studies in Keatsian women figures also reveal his longing for the ideal mother figure—to restore an infantile regressive fusing love. This finds extension in maternal figures like Cynthia, Isabella, Mnemosyne and even in a seductress like Circe.

So Keats's depiction of women figures in verse encompasses a wide range of conflicting attitudes. From approval of gender stereotypes, mother fixation to seeing women as 'valued other'—the attitudes also include other allied issues like narcissism, anxiety and suspicion. Other secondary issues which complicate Keats's attitude towards women are: his own hostility towards being marketed to women readers and his strong adverse criticism of leading contemporary women poets.

The psychological strands of Keats's insecure childhood and adolescence, contributed a great deal to his complex attitude towards women later in life. As I have discussed in chapter 1 of my book, biographical details of Keats's life help us to probe some of the complexities that recur in the female figures we find in his verse. Various circumstances in his childhood contributed to Keats's diffidence and anxiety in interaction with women. Besides unavoidable circumstances and an insecure childhood, several other factors socially isolated Keats the poet and sowed the seeds of gender confusion in his poetic psyche. The other factors include Keats's low social origin and gross flouting of the rigid codes of gender, both in characterization and poetic style. This marginalization indirectly aligned Keats with the otherwise ignored women poets of the Romantic period. That there is a remarkable degree of gender confusion and anxiety in Keats has become more evident especially in the light of recent criticism. Keats the poet threatened the conventional cultural constructions of masculinity, not only through iconoclastic characterizations of both male and female figures in his verse but also through recurrent revelations of conflicting attitudes in his letters, in his definition of negative capability, in being marketed exclusively to female readership and for several other factors.

In Keats's depiction of women figures in verse, we witness a wide gamut of complex male attitudes. These range from internalization or identification of self with women figures to adhering to conventional gender stereotypes of meek submissive or seductress female figures. In Chapter IV of my dissertation, I have explored the conventional female stereotype of meek helpless womanhood, through the central women figures Psyche, Madeline and Isabella. These meek helpless women figures are all cruelly trapped in a male dominated society.

I have also examined how Keats internalizes the female figure Psyche and aligns himself with the opposite sex. I have also explored Keats's depiction of seductresses of fatal women figures in verse, in the form of La Belle, Lamia and Melancholy. A wide range of diverging issues converge here, as Keats combines issues of autonomy, independence and free will of women with contrary conventional projections of gender stereotype in the form of aggressive seductress female figures. In a female figure like La Belle, as I have pointed out, the feminine perspective is ignored totally, with the patriarchal voices of authority silencing the female. Lamia reaffirms how a sexually conscious and assertive woman is a ruthlessly suppressed victim of patriarchal authority. Besides the issue of conventional gender stereotype of a seductress, *Lamia*, also explores the issue of sexual ambiguity. In Melancholy we find Keats defying conventional stereotypes of a seductress to grant the central woman figure a great deal of autonomy, independence, power, serenity and self-control. Keats here consciously departs from conventional norms to create an independent women.

Though chronologically an earlier work, Keats's *Endymion* is more complex and interesting in its exploration of femininity. *Endymion* compresses all male attitudes which appear separately in other poems. In Chapter V, I have discussed how Keats shows a gradual transformation from an idealistic, narcissistic and parochial vision of femininity to a broad based, altruistic and realistic one in *Endymion*. What is indeed amazing to observe is that in his later works instead of adhering to his final realization of woman as a 'valued other,' Keats once again returns to his journey of exploring the various strands of femininity. It reveals the brooding introspective nature of Keats the poet. As to whether it is a failure or not on part of Keats to adhere to an enlightened realization of femininity is a different issue altogether. However, even after the acceptance of the Indian maiden, Keats goes on to create liberated women figures in Moneta and Melancholy, but in the process of doing so, he also explores a wide range of conflicting gender issues in Psyche, La Bella, Isabella, Lamia and other female characters.

The triumph of Keats's poetic craftsmanship lies in this reluctance towards inferring, prescribing or imposing definite conclusions on readers. On the contrary, Keats's ability to explore, brood, experiment and probe into the various complex issues of gender in verse accounts for his triumph in poetic craftsmanship. He does not advocate or prescribe a definite perspective as regards gender in Romantic poetic discourse. His verse remains a witness to an intricate network of gender issues and various complex circumstances which shaped it. Keats's exploration of peripheral issues involving gender also abound in contraries, embodying subtle gender politics that time and again, tries to silence the female voice in Romantic poetic discourse.

Contraries prevail in the treatment of other peripheral issues related to gender in Keatsian verse. Nature as we all know, is a recurrent predominant theme in Romantic verse. Feminist critics[4] argue that though Nature has been engendered as feminine in poetic discourse and though her power is recognized; yet the conventional male Romantic poet is accused quite often of wresting, 'Nature's power, leaving her silenced, even absent'[5] from poetic discourse. Though Nature is gendered as 'Mother Earth, Dame Nature, Lady Bountiful,'[6] yet it is quite often an object of possession—an impediment that thwarts the male poet from becoming divine and has to be assimilated by any means. So much so, that nature is often silenced and she is bereft of her voice—the male Romantic poet speaks on her behalf. Even Keats displays this conventional male attitude. *In Ode on a Grecian Urn*, he engenders the urn as a female ('Thou still unravished bride of quietness') and after penetrating the world of beauty the female is silenced again, after being possessed, absorbed and assimilated. The female is silenced, as the poet says:

> Thou, silent form, dost tease us out of thought
> As doth eternity, Cold pastoral!
> When old age shall this generation waste,
> Thou shalt remain, in midst of other woe
> Than ours, a friend to man, to whom thou say'st,
> 'Beauty is truth, truth beauty'—that is all
> Ye know on earth, all ye need to know

[*Ode on a Grecian Urn*, V, 44-50]

It requires the male poet to articulate the 'silent form,' 'the bride of quietness.'

Even the apparently simple ode, *Ode to Autumn*, is not free of subtle gender politics. As Anne Mellor rightly points out,

> …Autumn, a season Keats originally gendered feminine in his letter to Reynold ("Chaste weather Dian skies") is rewritten as ambiguously androgynous, as both female gleaner and male reapers in Keats's great ode. Keats thus subtly empowers the male poet to utter the music of a female other, to become the voice of autumn and translate here "mellow fruitfulness" into his own consciousness of mutability and that "ripeness to the core" which enables him to accept the coming winter and his own death.[7]

Even in *Ode to a Nightingale*, the bird is engendered as female ['That thou, light winged Dryad (or female nymph) of the trees'] and is absorbed by the male poet. The beauty and charm of the nightingale's song cannot be transformed or decoded into the poet's language and so at the end of the poem,

> ….. 'tis buried deep
> In the next valley—glades.
>
> [*Ode to a Nightingale*, VIII, 77-78]

Thus it leaves 'the forlorn but speaking poet to interpret her meaning to his male audience.'[8]

> Here, where men sit and hear each other groan;
> Where palsy shakes a few, sad, last gray hairs.
>
> [*Ode to a Nightingale*, III, 24-25]

It is the male poet that ultimately relates the charm of the song to the male audience.

> Was it a vision, or a waking dream?
> Fled is that music….Do I wake or sleep?
>
> [*Ode to a Nightingale*, VIII, 79-80]

Such silencing of the female voice reminds us of Keats's *La Belle Dame Sans Merci*, where too the lady's perspective is totally ignored. We only get the male version of the tale with the knight relating his story to a patriarchal society who spontaneously sympathize with him and condemn and criticize the lady as a merciless seducer. Thus, we see how subtle gender politics operate in silencing the female voice in Romantic discourse, Keats is no exception to this phenomena.

Though the study of Keatsian women figures baffles us and prevents us from arriving at any definite conclusion about Keats, yet it provides a unique and interesting probe into the intricacies and complexities as to how the poetic mind works, especially when it comes to relationship with opposite sex. In her essay '*Feminising Keats*,' Susan J. Wolfson observes,

> ...For readings of Keats in the language of gender by Keats himself, by his contemporaries, and by his critics—typically set into play conflicts and contradicitions, the signifiance of which abides more in their persistent irresolution than in any possibility of a unified interpretation.[9]

Such conflicts, complexities, contradictions and ambiguities abound in Keats's depiction of female figures in verse. The traits of feminism that we find could well be due to the personal and social circumstances he faced in early nineteenth century society. Bereft of such socio-personal circumstances and marginalized existence, who knows in all probability, we would have witnessed a rather conventional attitude from Keats, like any other male Romantic poet. However, that is merely a hypothetical proposition. Whatever may be the reasons, Keats occupies a unique position in Romantic discourse, especially when it comes to portraying female figures in his verse. His attitude—as I have stated repeatedly—is not only unique, but complex as well, for various reasons. At the end, it can be said that Keats's special case defies any form of classification—especially as regards his attitude towards the opposite sex. An observation firmly established now, especially through a close study of the female figures we encounter in his verse.

NOTES

1. Susan J. Wolfson, Margaret Homans, Anne K. Mellor. Marjorie Levinson and others.

2. Anne K. Mellor, *Romanticism & Gender* (London & New York: Routedge, 1993) p. 171.
3. Wolfson, Homans, Mellor and others.
4. Anne K. Mellor, Karen Swann and others.
5. Mellor, *op. cit.*, p. 18.
6. Mellor, *op. cit.*, p. 21.
7. Mellor, *op. cit.*, p. 21.
8. Mellor, *op. cit.*, p. 21.
9. Susan J. Wolfson, *Feminising Keats* in Peter J. Kitson ed. *New Casebooks*: *Coleridge. Keats and Shelley*. (London: Macmillan Press Ltd. 1996) p. 109.

Bibliography

Texts

Allott Miriam, ed. *The Poems of John Keats,* 1970: corr. rpt. London: Longman Group Ltd., 1980.

Cook, Elizabeth, ed. *The Oxford Authors: John Keats* Oxford: Oxford University Press, 1990.

Gittings Robert, ed. *Letters of John Keats*, 1970; corr. rpt. Oxford: Oxford University Press, 1986.

Rollins, Hyder Edward, ed. *The Keats Circle; Letters and Papers and More Letters and Poems of the Keats Circle.* 1948: rpt. Cambridge, Mass achusetts: Harvard University Press, 1965, 2 Vols.

Rollins Hyder Edward, ed. *The Letters of John Keats.* 1814-1821, Cambridge.

Rollins Hyder Edward, ed. Massachusetts: Harvard University Press 1958, 2 Vols.

Stillinger Jack, ed. *The Poems of John Keats* London: Heinemann 1978.

Biography

Bate Walter Jackson, *John Keats* London: Chatto & Windus 1979.

Coote Stephen, *John Keats, A Life.* London Hodder and Stoughton 1995.

Gittings Robert, *John Keats* 1968: rpt. Middlesex: Penguin Books Ltd., 1985.

Ward Aileen, *John Keats: The Making of a Poet,* 1963: rpt. Canada: Collins Publishers Toronto 1986.

Criticism and Background

Abrams M.H., *The Mirror and the Lamp: Romantic Theory and the Critical Tradition* 1953: rpt. Oxford: Oxford University Press, 1971. *A Glossary of Literary Terms* 6th edn. 1957. Bangalore Prism Books Pvt. Ltd., & Harcourt Brace & Co., USA 1993. ed., English Romantic Poets: Modern Essays in Criticism, New York: Oxford University Press, 1975.

Aske Martin, *Keats and Hellenism*: An Essay, Cambridge: Cambrigde University Press 1985.

Barth Robert J. and Mahoney, L. John, ed. *Coleridge Keats and the Imagination: Romanticism and Adam's Dream Essays in Honour of W.J. Bate* Columbia : University of Missouri Press, 1990.

Barnard John, *John Keats,* Cambridge: Cambridge University Press, 1987.

Bayley John, *Keats and Reality* British Academy Leacture, 1962.

Bennet Andrew, *Keats Narrative and Audience: The Posthumous Life of Writing* Cambridge: Cambridge University Press, 1994.

Beyer Werner William, Keats and the Daemon King New York: Octagon, 1969.

Bloom Harold, *The Visionary Company: A Reading of English Romantic Poetry,* 1961; rpt. New York: Cornell University Press, 1971.

Bouce Paul Gabriel, ed. *Sexuality in Eighteenth Century Britain,* Manchester University Press, 1982.

Bush Douglas, *John Keats: His Life and Writings* London: Weiderfeld and Nicolson, 1966.

Clarke Bruce, *Fabulous Monsters of Conscience: Anthropomorphosis in Keats's Lamia* Si R. 23 (1984), 555-79.

Chatterjee Bhabatosh, *John Keats: His Mind and Work* Bombay: Orient Longman.1971.

Chatterjee Lola, *Woman—Image—Text: Feminist Readings of Literary Texts.* New Delhi Trianka 1986.

D'Avanzo Mario I., *Keats's Metaphors for the Poetic Imagination,* 1967 rpt. Durham, N.C., Duke University Press, 1971.

Dickstein Morris., *Keats and His Poetry: A Study in Development,* Chicago: University of Chicago Press, 1971.

Empson William, *Seven Types of Ambiguity,* 1930 rpt London: Penguin Books Ltd., 1995.

Ende Stuart A, *Keats and the Sublime,* New Haven Yale University Press. 1976.

Enscoe Gerald, *Eros and the Romantics: Sexual Love as a theme in Coleridge, Shelley and Keats* Hague Netherlands: Mouton & Co. N.V. Publishers, 1967.

Ever Walter, *Aesthetic and Myth in the Poetry of Keats* Princeton N.J.: Princeton University Press, 1965.

Ferguson Mary Anne, *Images of Women in Literature* 2nd ed., Boston: Houghton Mifflin, 1977.

Finney Claude Lee, *The Evolution of Keats's Poetry* Cambridge Mass: Harvard University Press 1936, 2 Vols.

Fraser George Sutherland, ed. John *Keats: Odes. A Casebook* London: Macmillan Press 1971.

Gittings Robert, *The Keats Inheritance London:* Heinemann, 1964.

Gittings Robert, *John Keats: The Living Year,* London: Heinemann, 1954.

Goellnicht, Donald C., *The Poet—Physician Keats and Medical Science,* Pittsburgh: University of Pittsburgh Press, 1984.

Goldberg Milton Allan, *The Poetics of Romanticism: Towards a Reading of John Keats,* Ohio, Antioch 1969.

Goodman Lizbeth, ed. *Literature and Gender,* London: Routledge & The Open University, 1996.

Gorell Lord, *John Keats: The Principle of Beauty,* Folcroft Press,1970.

Harrison G.B., *A Book of English Poetry,* 1937: rpt. Middlesex Penguin 1983.

Hill John Spencer, ed. *Keats: The Narrative Poems, A Casebook* London & Basing stoke: Macmillan Press, 1983.

Jack Ian, *Keats and the Mirror of Art* Oxford: Clarendon Press, 1967.

Jones John, *John Keats's Dream of Truth,* London: Chatto & Windus, 1969.

Jones Vivien, *Women in the Eighteenth Century: Constructions of Feminity,* London: Routledge 1990.

Kitson Peter J., *New Casebooks: Caleridge Keats and* Shelley, London: Macmillan Press, 1996.

La Gory Michael, *Wormy Circumstance: Symbolism in Keats's Isabella* Sir Vol., 34 No. 3, 1995, 321-342.

Levison Marjorie. *Keats's Life of Allegory: The Origins of a Style,* 1988: rpt. Oxford: Basil Blackwell, 1990.

Little Judy, *Keats as a Narrative Poet: A Test of Invention* Lincoln: University of Nebraska Press, 1975.

Mathews G.M., ed. *Keats: The Critical Heritage* 1971: rpt. London, New York: Routledge, 1975.

Mayhead Robin, *John Keats* Cambridge: Cambridge University Press, 1967.

Mellor Anne K., *Romanticism & Gender* London & New York: Routledge, 1993 *Romanticism & Feminism,* Bloomington: Indian University Press, 1988.

Mill John Stuart, *On Liberty, Representative Government The Subjection of Women,* London: Oxford University Press, 1933.

Millett Kate, *Sexual Politics,* London: Rupert Hart Davis/Grander Publishing 1971.

Muir Kenneth, ed. *John Keats: A Reassessment,* 1958 rpt. Liverpool University Press, 1969.

Murry John Middleton, *Keats and Shakespeare,* London: Oxford University Press, 1926.

Murry John Middleton, *Keats,* London: Jouathan Cape, 1955.

Murry John Middleton, *Studies in Keats,* Oxford: Oxford University Press, 1930.

O'Neill Judith, ed. *Critics on Keats,* London: George Allen and Unwin Ltd., 1967.

Pinion F.B., *A Keats Chronology,* London: Macmillan Press, 1992.

Ricks Christopher, *Keats and Embarrassment,* Oxford: Clarender Press, 1974.

Ridley M.R., *Keats's Craftsmanship: A Study in Poetic Development,* 1933: Rpt. London: Methuen, 1965.

Roe Nicholas, *John Keats and the Culture of Dissent,* Oxford: Clarendon Press, 1997.

Roe Nicholas, *Keats's Lisping Sedition* in Kitson Peter J. ed. *New Casebooks: Coleridge Keats and Shelley,* London: Macmillan Press, 1996.

Ryan Robert M., *Keats: The Religious Sense,* Princeton NJ: Princeton University Press, 1976.

Rezepka Charles J., *The Self as Mind: Vision and Identity in Wordsworth, Coleridge and Keats,* Cambridge Mass: Harvard University Press, 1986.

Schapiro Barbara A., *The Romantic Mother: Narcissistic Patterns in Romantic Poetry,* Baltimore: John Hopkins University Press, 1983.

Sharp Ronald A., *Keats, Skepticism and the Religion of Beauty,* Athens: University of Georgia Press, 1979.

Sperry Stuart M., *Keats the Poet* NJ: Princeton University Press, 1973. The *Allegory of Endymion* in Hill Spencer ed. Keats I, *The Narrative Poems A Casebook,* London: Macmillan 1983, 81-104. Also in *Keats the Poet,* Chapter 4, 90-116.

Spurgeon Caroline Frances, Keats's Shakespeare: *A Descriptive Study,* Oxford: Clarendor Press, 1966.

Stillinger Jack, *The Hood winking of Madeline Scepticism in The Eve of St Agnes* in Spencer Hill ed. Keats: The Narrative Poems, London: Macmillan Press, 1983, 144-167.

Stone Brian, *The Poetry of Keats,* London: Penguin 1992 Mellor Anne K. ed.

Swann Karen, *Harassing the Muse* in Mellor, Anne K. ed. *Romanticism and Feminism* Bloomington: Indiana University Press, 1988, 81-92.

Van Ghent Dorothy, *Keats: The Myth of the Hero,* New Jersey: Princeton University Press, 1983.

Vendler Helen, *The Odes of John Keats,* Cambridge Mass: Belknap Press, Harvard University, 1983.

Waldoff Leon, *Keats and the Silent Work of Imagination,* Urbana: University of Illinois Press, 1985.

Wasserman Earl.R., *The Finer Tone: Keats's Major Poems* 1953: rpt. Baltimore: The John Hopkins Press, 1960.

Watts Cedric, *A Preface to Keats,* 1985 rpt. Singapore Publishers, 1993.

White R.S., *Keats as a Reader of Shakespeare,* London: Athlone Press, 1987.

Wolfson Susan J, *Feminising Keats* in Kitson Peter J. ed. *New Casebooks Coleridge Keats and Shelley* London: Macmillan 1996, 92-113.

Woolfe Virginia, *A Room of One's Own,* 1929: rpt. London & Toronto: The Hogarth Press Ltd. & Irwin Co., 1949.

